ONE MILE
BELOW
BOTTOM
KEEPING YOUR JOY
IN HELL

Denisha N. Tate

ONE MILE BELOW BOTTOM – KEEPING YOUR JOY IN HELL

ISBN: 978-1-949826-00-5 (paperback)
ISBN: 978-1-949826-01-2 (e-book)

Library of Congress Control Number: 2018911761

Edited by: Tecia Sellers
Exterior cover design by: Ewa Henry
Interior design by: Anita "AC" Clinton

Published by: Eagles Global Publishing

More about the author: www.DenishaLeads.com

DEDICATION

This book is dedicated to:

My God who comforted me in the depths of my pain and revealed Himself to me in ways that words cannot explain.

My village. Without you, I would not be. Thank you for your prayers, words of encouragement, support, and belief in me. Your faith became my strength. Your love keeps me alive.
LIVE LOVE

TABLE OF CONTENTS

INTRODUCTION

ONE MILE BELOW BOTTOM – KEEPING YOUR JOY IN HELL

Life will provide you markers to document your journey from here to there. You must decide where you are going.

There are feet and inch markers to tell you how tall you have grown. There are water level meters to let you know how high the water has risen. There are mile markers to let you know how far you have traveled. But what type of marker tells you how deep in hell you have fallen?

You see, no one plans to fall. When jumping out of a plane, you put on a parachute. But when life happens, and you forget to pack your chute – what then? Free falling is only fun when you have a harness and know that it won't result in your demise. What marker should one prepare to read on the descend into the pit?

FALLING...

To become good at something, a person must practice repeatedly. How does one become good at disappointment? How does one master the let down? What training has been developed for bad news that will not end?

Truth be told, life! Life can prepare you to take a gut punch and a slap in the face without blinking. Or maybe just MY life. We all have problems of one variety or another. But have you ever felt like you could not get a reprieve? Have you longed for just a moment of peace? Can the bad news take one day off? Really? For me, that is what it feels like to fall... continuously.

JOY...

Allow me to share with you the concept of 'markers' and how they play a vital role in my life of survival and hope! I have been trained to find the good news despite the circumstance. I had to. If not, I would have exited this planet by now. No! Self-inflicted endings were never going to be my style. I had too much to live for, at least I hoped.

I have been called a medical miracle. Others have marveled at my ability to always seem joyful. Truth be told, I can honestly say that I do not look anything like what I have gone through! If you do not believe me, let me tell you!

Wait, I do not want to get ahead of myself.

Markers of joy became my saving grace. I learned to search for the positive, chart progress, and acknowledge forward movement- regardless of span. This became useful as life's circumstances hurt me to the core. In pain, but still able to find my joy.

MARKERS...

While unpacking a box of promotional materials, I came across a pedometer. Counting steps? I invested in a pedometer and then realized that I wasted my money. I gave it away as a gift. The concept of counting my steps was a microtask that proved unproductive to me. Steps? I needed my markers to be more substantial, cover more ground.

Markers remind me of my little sister. She once tracked her height on the wall in her bedroom. There was no goal, it was simply to document her growth. I saw no point in this activity, nonetheless I cherished the experience with her. She stood still, neck stretched out, waiting with excitement for the new mark. "Am I taller, how much did I grow?" she would ask.

It was as if each new marker brought her joy. We would discuss her markers of joy. Her excitement was unbelievable. She would go on and on about her height. Any amount of growth made her happy. More importantly, me experiencing this with her, witnessing her growth, is a fond memory for us both.

Not all markers bring joy. My memory of a personal marker was that on the outdoor track. Four laps around the track equaled one mile. At the beginning of my wellness journey, my trainer began with the goal of me completing the one mile walk with ease. The first day of training was a turning point in my life. It challenged my self-image and my identity. I failed. I could not walk the mile. By the end of 100 meters, I felt my heart pounding in my ears. I could not catch my breath. I felt as if I was going to pass out. I was supposed to complete 1600 meters with ease? I thought to myself, "I cannot do it!" This was my declaration of defeat. I was angry! I went home a failure, a quitter, a loser. I did not want to look in the mirror. This blob of a person was pitiful and worthless! One mile became my marker of accomplishment or lack thereof! This distance represented a gap as far as the east is from the west. Impossibility for sure.

Prior to this point, I was proud of my accomplishments. I was a leader and admired by many. But now, I was in unfamiliar territory. Doubt, fear, low self-esteem? None of this was me! How did I end up here? I could not stay here! A few days later, I went back to the track. I was embarrassed, disempowered, and afraid. "What if I cannot do it? Have I really lost control of my life to the point of being too obese to walk a mile with ease? What kind of loser have I become?" Were all questions in my mind. The voice in my head became my biggest enemy. That self-doubt lasted until I was joined by a friend on the journey. She was determined to reset her health as well. By my third week, I had built up endurance to complete one full lap of the required four. I was sweating and exhausted, but I had accomplished my 400-meter hurdle. I only had 1200 to go! I had not accomplished the goal, but I made progress. I was beginning to feel hopeful. I was grateful to have someone join me. Maybe we could encourage one another. Or maybe, I could have someone agree with me on my days of defeat, "Yes, this is stupid." There are approximately 2,000 steps in one mile. When you are weighted down, broken, exhausted, and drained, simply taking the first step seems impossible, let alone 2,000! But I will not give up!

From that point forward, any task that seemed impossible was labeled as MY MILE. By the way, I eventually walked the mile, ran the mile, and can complete 4 miles without breaking a sweat. I did not believe it was possible. Every step, every meter, every lap led me to my success. I needed markers along the way, to keep me inspired. I now understood my little sister's excitement. It was the progress that brought her joy, not the ending. The journey along the way fueled her hope which kept her inspired. I just needed to focus on the markers of progress.

So what role do markers play in hell? When everything is going wrong and you have already experienced your "one more thing" moment. You know what that is. You tell the universe, "if one more thing happens I'm going to...," you fill in the blank. At that moment, when the bricks of misfortune are piling high, the markers play a pivotal role. Honestly, you decide what they reveal to you. There will be interruptions to your situation.

You determine the lens in which you view each marker. Will you take a breath during the storm or are you going to drown? When walking on a stairwell, you decide whether to go up or go down. The stairs do not change, they are constant. You decide based upon your desired destination. Markers work the same way. They are simply snapshots at a moment in time. The energy given to the marker comes from you. A blessing or a curse, is up to you.

You endure the test so that you can share your testimony. Yes, I have been to hell and back. I may even smell like smoke, but I did not burn!

If you want to end the pain, reshape your lens, and find your joy, I can help. Allow me to guide you through identifying your markers of joy. They are there, can you see them? **ONE MILE BELOW BOTTOM** will guide you out of the pit created by your pain and reveal the markers of joy waiting to be uncovered along the journey. You too can learn to **KEEP YOUR JOY IN HELL.**

ONE MILE
BELOW
BOTTOM
KEEPING YOUR JOY
IN HELL

CHAPTER 1
HITTING ROCK BOTTOM

Rock bottom is a destination you define. It is personal and intimate. There is a welcome sign in your handwriting when you arrive!

As I look in the mirror, I do not recognize the person looking back at me. Where is her spark? Where is her glow? She looks like a lifeless shell of a person. Who is she? As tears roll down my face, I accept that she is me. How did we get here? And where is here?

As a kid, I experienced living on public assistance. I know what it is like to change residence several times. I even understand the need for sacrifice of the "nice to have" items to ensure you take care of the "have to have" list. I am not afraid of hard times. I know how to survive difficult times, trust me.

But this was something different. I have arrived at a place that haunted me in my nightmares. I am at a place that always caused me fear. I am at the place of uncertainty. Not knowing the plan scares me like nothing else! I remember when this fear developed. It was during my childhood. We left in a hurry after a major fight. "Mommy where are we going? What happened?" I asked as we drove away. My little brother and I were in the car, but my papa was not. I did not feel safe because I was unsure of what was going on. Uncertainty scared me and would continue to do so for many years to come.

During my childhood, this scenario would play out again and this feeling would return. But eventually, I grew up and was now in control. I made sure I always knew what was going on and what my next move would be. Now that I was in control, I believed I would never deal with uncertainty again!

Many years later, I was at the funeral of a dear colleague. Much of the conversation before and after the services was about his career, and how his job really shaped his identity. Everyone shared humorous stories of various adventures with our dear friend. Although the gathering felt festive and inspiring, I was left with a nagging question. Apart from the job who was he? The question caused me to be introspective. Apart from the job who am I? I was not sure. I could not answer the question. Oh no, uncertainty. Apart from my job WHO AM I?

I realized that my job had become my soul identity. It was what I was known for. It was the lens in which all my decisions were viewed through. It became my name. "Oh yes, that is her from…" I belonged to it and I was proud!

This fusion process was not new to me. Historically, my identity was always linked to others. I was his daughter and her oldest child. I was their big sister and her best friend. I was accepted on their team and joined their sorority. And now for nearly 20 years, I had been one of them – I belonged. I was always sure of who I was. I am a member of the group.

Looking back, I have realized that it was fifth grade when I learned who I was to others. I was given the title that described me. Prior to this designation, I was labeled bossy and talkative. However, this time I was told that others listened to me and trusted me. I was considered popular. I was even told I had a good head on my shoulders and keen understanding. Honestly, I did not know what to make of those descriptions.

All those characteristics rolled together had a name. I was introduced to my new identity – leader. I WAS A LEADER. I am not just in the group. I lead the group! The title of leader carried responsibility, authority, and pressure. I owned it. I never put it down.

On the job, I was a leader, expert, coach, mentor, and guide. At least that is what people claimed. Very quickly, my personal identity became engulfed by my career and I loved it!

MOMENT OF TRUTH

Let me share a little secret. I must tell you the truth. Being a leader is not as glamorous as many make it out to be. As a matter of fact, being a leader is lonely, difficult, and scary at times. You wonder if you are making the right decisions. Leading is a commitment that includes putting others before yourself. You must accept that the whole is more important than your individual part. And most of all, as my good friend Andre always says, "leaders do not throw sand in the gears!" He constantly reminded others of their requirement to work with the team and not sabotage the group.

Up to this point, I was excited about my choices in life. I kept the promises that seven-year-old me made when no one was listening.

"When we grow up, we are going to have our own house. That way we do not have to keep moving. We are going to have our own car, so we do not have to ask anyone to take us anywhere. And we are going to have a job we love! We are going to go to work every day!"

Seven-year-old me was proud. We did it! This was the foundation of my hard wiring – The Promise. I approached every day looking for a way to improve my skills, enhance my team's impact, and increase the positive results of the company. It did not matter how many hours it took. I was having the time of my life! And that was my truth.

THE LOVE AFFAIR

None of this was done with the goal of receiving awards or having my name on a wall. I was more comfortable working behind the scenes, inspiring others, and pushing them higher. I led because I longed for progress and continual improvement, not to be recognized. I did, however, receive various honors. There were people inspired by my career and they considered me an expert in a few areas. This was humbling and energized me to keep moving.

If any of this sounds familiar, then you may be a workaholic. I am not passing judgement, simply stating an observation.

Contrary to the warnings of burnout and overload, I saw nothing wrong with my work habits. I was addicted. I longed to be the go-to girl. I loved to solve problems for others. I did not get wrapped up in who did what. A friend once told me, "problems are simply opportunities waiting to be uncovered." Lisa was right! I agreed with her wholeheartedly. I saw problems as opportunities. They were opportunities to stretch and grow. Opportunities to learn and innovate. Opportunities to save the day by making someone else's life easier. Yes, bring on the problems!

My grandma often said, "be careful what you ask for because you just might get it."

A normal week usually contained Sixty-Five or more hours spent on work tasks. This often included six-day work weeks. I loved what I was doing and could not get enough of it. I was in a love affair with my job.

This was not love at first sight. No, it was a slowly evolving love. You know what I mean. At first your attention is grabbed, but you do not give in to the feeling. Next you find yourself coming in for a closer view. Then the next thing you know-BAM- you are in love!

In the beginning, I found myself excited about learning. Each time I learned something new, I felt empowered. I volunteered for every pilot project available. I participated with pride. I found my place in the grand plan. I belonged and had purpose for the first time in my adult life!

The more I participated, the more opportunities to participate emerged. My network grew, my authority increased, and I was confident. I studied long hours and immersed myself in gaining as much knowledge as possible. I had mentors, sponsors, and guides throughout the entire process.

Like any relationship, there were bad days, but I quickly got over it and ran back asking for more. When I was away from work, it was on my mind. Everything around me reminded me of my job. New ideas would emerge during dinner. I would quickly write them down or call a colleague to share my new-found inspiration. There were no time parameters. An email at 3 am was normal. Sitting at my desk at 10 pm was too. I was willfully married to my career. Some referred to my job as, him. He (my job) became my number one. This love ran deep. If he needed anything, I would drop it all and run to him. I had no husband or children to compete with my job. I carried every coworker, team member, and client in my heart. We were a family.

We were a couple, and everyone knew it. Eventually, I did not know where I began, and the job ended. My preferences were developed through job interactions. My restaurant choice was rooted in an experience at a previous meeting there. My cities of travel on vacation began with an introduction from a job conference or seminar. My entertainment experiences were even tied to my beloved job. I was like a child who did not know what she liked. It was determined for me. At the time, I saw nothing wrong with it all. The choices were exciting. The exposure was first class and my life was like a dream. I was in love with my job and I did not care who knew it! He took great care of me.

My friends could not separate me from him. On the rare occasion, I would go on a non-work-related vacation, I found a way to bring him along with me. He was my everything. He completed me. A milestone in my life wasn't officially good until someone from my job affirmed it. My friendships were developed through my job. My community identity was tied to him. He opened doors for me and ensured that I had a seat at the table. Twenty years and four communities. I would follow him anywhere. I was in love and it felt amazing (except for when it was not). Let us not forget, I am talking about my job!

At this point, you may be confused or even concerned about my attachment to my job. Good! If you are not, or even better, if you understand me and can personally relate…warning – you my friend may have a problem. No offense, I am simply stating another observation.

While out to dinner with a friend, I heard the conversation at the table next to us. A lady was sharing how much she hated her job. She described waking every morning, dreading having to go to work. Her companion replied with horror stories of her own. She remarked, "the job would be ok if some of those people were not there!" They both laughed, but I do not believe either of them were joking. At that moment, I reflected, "what would I do if I felt that way?" I felt fortunate to not have to answer that question. Not that day anyway.

TO BE NEEDED

My style was described as a servant leader. I worked for the people that worked for me and together we worked for our clients. I took pride in making my people shine and they reciprocated by shining brightly. I attracted talent and required the best out of them. Together we could accomplish almost anything. This dynamic played a major role in my love affair with my job.

I realize that I was wired to be on a team. This was my natural inclination. As a youth, I had cousins and neighborhood friends that hung together like a little crew. I was never alone. In high school, my education track consisted of a self-contained group of 40 students that had been deemed as leadership potential, college bound, and full of promise. In college I joined a little sister organization that provided guidance and companionship as I navigated the new-found freedoms college provided. I pledged a Sorority before graduation and now, I have the dream job that allows me to be a part of something bigger than myself. This felt familiar, this dynamic was just right for me. I was on the team, leading the team, and needed the team.

As my career developed, I had role models that led through a team approach. There was one occasion that cemented in my mind what it felt like to be one with a group of people. Our President informed the team that we were to attend an upcoming event being hosted by a major partner. Everyone was given their assignments. We were going to work the room. New friends, potential partners, future ambassadors, our targets were set.

The event day came, and I vividly remember feeling like an athlete prepared for the big game. I was excited, nervous, and determined to make my leader proud. I would show up for my team! We carpooled from the office and had been laughing and joking on the journey. It was a beautiful sunny day and the ride increased my anticipation. As we arrived, the room buzzed with energy. We walked in like a team of superheroes. Our President walked in first, and we followed two by two in a sort of V formation. It was not choreographed or planned. We were simply in sync and floated through the room as if we owned that moment! And yes, there was music playing, maybe just in my head, but a theme song was truly appropriate. I was on the power team and I loved it! From that point forward, I knew that characteristic was going to be a part of my leadership tool belt. We would be in sync. We would be one!

As I led teams, I created oneness. To be clear, I am not talking about clones. No, this is synergy at its finest. Imagine going to work with a team that represented various components of yourself. Sitting next to me was a person that shared my strategic thought process but had a creativity that was mind blowing. Across from them was a person that understood my heart and love for people and seemed to know everyone in town. At the end of the table was a person with the sarcasm to remind us all the no one is perfect, especially not in this room. And everyone believed in the mission and hard work. Each day was easy. Not because of simplistic tasks or minor challenges. The days were easy because we understood each other. We spoke the same language. We all saw success the same way. We also respected one another for our differences in addition to our similarities. This made me love my job even more. Every team I led and participated on merged to become something better than the parts alone. Synergy is represented as 1+1=3. Not for us! For us it was 1+1= infinity. We were super as a unit.

When fighting in a war, victory is that much easier if you can avoid internal conflict during the battle. No friendly fire here. We needed each other, and we took this very seriously.

Team meetings were like Sunday family dinners. There were a multitude of topics discussed. There were several elephants uncovered and dismissed from the room. There were questions and push-back along the way. We laughed and even got loud on occasion. In the end, decisions were made, and problems were solved. We left the room with a plan of action, responsibilities clearly outlined, and the details of "good enough" was a vision shared by all. We were a team!

I knew that as a leader it was important to be a part of the team I was leading. It is a delicate balance to not become a peer yet remain together with the group. When you genuinely care about your people this can be a challenge. There must be boundaries, clear expectations, and accountability. We respected this balance. We all wanted to win- not for the win alone, but for each other. We celebrated births, weddings, divorces, new loves, kids, graduations, and home goings. We experienced it all – together. We loved each other. I loved my job!

Relationships are important in business. The people you know are important. However, what those people know about you, can open doors. When you have a team of ambassadors, your name will enter conversations without you being in the room. Opportunities are uncovered by those who know you and believe in you.

My love affair has introduced me to hundreds of people who have become close friends. Each city provided an opportunity to join new teams, inspire additional people, and uncover greater opportunities. My family was massive, and my reputation was growing by leaps and bounds. I was loved. This further reinforced my love affair. To love and be loved in return was a dream come true.

BRANDED

The last component of my love relationship with my job was that of branding. My company had an impressive brand. The goal was to not only become a trusted name in the community, but to become a household name of choice. We were on the path of something great! The company believed that great work was to be acknowledged, celebrated, and supported. I had the pleasure of participating in modern day miracles. Imagine identifying your life's purpose, finding a job that aligned with that purpose, and being allowed to live that purpose to its full extent, every day. That my friend was called "my life." I had arrived. It did not feel like work.

I even developed a full wardrobe that displayed the company logo. Shirts, polos, scarves, hats, bags, even jewelry adorned my person. I was always recognizable as affiliated with my love. I was branded. It was as if the logo was my diamond ring of commitment. I proudly represented our union. I was not the lady in the restaurant lamenting with a friend about how I hate my job. That was not my story. I can handle whatever problem comes my way. I am in love.

THE RUB

There are people who face life from opposing philosophies. Neither is right or wrong. They are simply different and a better fit for the individual's style. There are times when those differences can cause a rub. You must be careful to not cross the wires that will cause a short circuit. The trick however is to know which wires not to cross.

I choose to face each day with the mindset of possibility and optimism. Growing up, my life was filled with music. My mom always had the radio playing and we would sing along. I have many fond memories of Saturday clean up. The smell of cleaning solution, a fresh breeze blowing, and a song in the air. My life has a soundtrack. I can hear a song and instantly be transported back to a happy day of my youth. That experience usually makes me smile.

My facial expression is that of joy. I smile often. I smile at people as they pass by. I smile when holding a conversation on the phone. I even smile when driving down the street. For one, it makes me feel good. But it is also something I can give others. People seem to enjoy receiving a smile. Most people give me one back! Smiles cross language barriers, color lines, age definitions, and economic statuses.

My job kept me smiling. Daily accomplishments of those around me, brought such joy and moments of hope. Like anyone in love, I found myself smiling most of the time.

I remember the day my smiling became the topic of discussion.

While walking down the hall, a coworker stopped me in my tracks by asking, "Why are you always smiling? Who has that much to smile about?" The question caused me a moment of pause. I did not know how to answer that question. Prior to this moment, I had not thought about my daily smile quota. I did not realize that I smiled too often. I was aware of my joy, but I had not thought about my facial expression being considered excessive. I shrugged my shoulders and walked away. As I was walking to my office, I looked back. She stood there shaking her head as I thought to myself, "Wait, she really wanted an answer?" I was confused as to why this question surfaced. I began to wonder if my smiling really caused a problem. If so, why? Do I smile too much? What does this mean? I was confused. Maybe it is because I was in love. Is this a rub?

Later that week, I was in a discussion with another colleague. As our meeting ended he stated, "you know you care too much." I was unclear of the context of his comment. I asked, "what do you mean?" He then explained that he had no specific example; but he wanted to share this concern with me.

First, I smiled too much and now I care too much. What is going on around here? Has there been a change and I missed the memo? I thought to myself- love makes you smile and you care when you are in love. They simply do not get it.

I listened to the constructive feedback. As months passed, these two conversations haunted me. They were more than just thought provoking. This was a rub. I became self-conscious. I became concerned. I found myself uncertain.

Imagine being in a loving relationship and someone plants the seed that maybe things are not as you think they are. You may ignore it at first, but eventually you begin to wonder. Once the wondering begins, you subconsciously assess every moment to ensure you have not been missing signs that are right before your eyes. Love can make you blind and no one wants to be love's fool!

I did what any enlightened being would do. I began to change! I stopped smiling as much. I made sure that I was not being too emotional or caring. I remember thinking, "Wow, this is harder than I thought. I guess I do smile too much. I had to stop myself from smiling at least ten times in the past few hours."

When a "rub" occurs, it is important to get clarification. What did the other person mean? Why did they ask or say what they did? What is the depth of their perspective? Is their perspective right for my life? If you fail to get clarification, you can find yourself reacting to a commentary that was never yours, but the consequences will be yours and yours alone.

From that point forward, something felt different. It was as if my love asked a question that changed the entire dynamic of our relationship. I am smiling less and withdrawing a bit. But wait, why? I never knew why, but it felt like the right thing to do. I did not want to make anyone uncomfortable, especially not my love. If my job wants me to tone it down, I will.

NEW NORMAL

This particular Monday felt like it dragged on forever. The meetings seemed longer and the mood around the office was less festive than normal. Or maybe I had changed. I was less festive. It is Monday, so this is normal, right?

The line that normally formed outside my office, now found a closed door most of the time. If someone knocked, I would welcome them in. But I needed to provide space. I needed to tone it down. I was doing my best to follow the advice I was given.

After work, I went out for dinner. I hoped my table was available. Now that I think about it, I had been eating out often. My clothes were fitting differently. When did I get "my" table? Changes were occurring for sure.

Over time, this new normal had a negative impact on my life. Eating out not only cost hundreds of dollars weekly, I now tipped the scale in the category identified as obese by our health insurance carrier. "I smile too much, I care too much, and now I am fat! Really, what else is wrong with me?"

I should have never asked. The answer to this question became my quest. I received daily entries for the list of wrongs needing attention. I began to take things personally. I began to feel like a failure. On the outside, I worked harder. I spent more time helping others. I volunteered for every task available. But inside I was chasing a question, "What is wrong with me?" I will not live in uncertainty. I can handle the truth. I just need to know. I had to know.

One Wednesday, while participating in a meeting, I presented information to my colleagues. Someone asked a question and I instantly felt a knot in the pit of my stomach. "Did I say something wrong? Was my information not accurate?" I slowly and tentatively replied to the inquiry. My co-worker thanked me. He was reviewing his notes and could not read his own writing. He wanted to make sure he had the correct information for his team.

"What a relief!" I felt better knowing I had not embarrassed myself. My hands were shaking slightly, and my pulse was racing. I had prepared myself for the worst. Gladly, I was wrong. The meeting finally ended, and I was free. This was one example of how my new insecurities surfaced in the workplace.

This downward spiral was more than a bad day or a moment of low esteem. It became toxic stress and trauma. I felt as if my joy was too much, so I hid it. I felt my kindness was a weakness, so I withdrew. I was self-conscious of every decision I made. I spent hours researching, fact checking, and gaining consensus. I did not want to mess anything up. I became unsure of myself. I could not identify the source of my confidence declining. I just did not trust myself as much as I once did.

I spent many evening meals contemplating my current mindset. The contemplating was showing up in pounds. Clearly, I was deep in thought, at least my scale seemed to think so.

In addition to being obese, I also suffered from muscle spasms. These incidents ranged from mild ticks to noticeable contortions that mimicked a stroke episode. I had now experienced one ambulance ride and two additional hospital visits.

The doctor looked me in the eye and said, "Ma'am, stress is dangerous and with your current weight, eating habits, long work hours, and sleep issues there needs to be a change." I looked him in the eyes and tried to hold back my tears. I thought to myself, "Something had changed. I have changed. I was in trouble and I did not know how to fix it. My source of joy, support, companionship, and purpose was turning on me. Nothing seemed familiar. I felt out of place. I really like my job, but my job is killing me, slowly."

Over time, I trained myself to work through the sickness. I came to work in pain. I put on a happy face (but not too happy) and kept forging ahead. I was good at my job. This was my life's purpose. I could not stop now! They need me, and I need them. This job is my family and my life. Who am I outside these walls?

In a relationship, the couple develops their friends network. These people belong to you both. Your identity is a composite of the two of you. If someone encounters you alone, they instantly ask you where the other half is. Not only was I unclear of my personal identity. I truly did not plan on figuring out which of us got to keep the friends. That was unthinkable.

I spent several evenings contemplating my future. Is this going to be my forever? Is this going to work for me? I was constantly sick in my body. I was unhappy. I noticed that others felt unhappy too. Was my ability to inspire failing? It is difficult to provide what you lack.

I had options. My love had not abandoned me. I received offers to move to other cities and continue my career. But for some reason, the offer to move was not appealing. Previously, my love pointed me to new cities and I packed without hesitation. Today, was not the day of retreat. I had something else in store, I just did not understand what. Honestly, I was terrified that my life was ending. I heard the doctor and I believed him; stress will kill you. I did not want to die!

IN PLAIN SIGHT

I was in crisis. My joy was gone but I was unsure where I lost it. My health was deteriorating, and I knew it. Joylessness was spreading, and I could not stop it. I was on a freefall with no parachute and I could not catch my breath. My deterioration was apparent and in plain sight. The dark circles under my eyes, the excessive weight gain, and the diminished joy was obvious.

Once a week, I had something to look forward to. I attended Tuesday Bible study. I found peace in my house of worship. I thought, if I could spend some time in my church, I could get centered and find North again. I left the office and headed to the church. I would arrive in less than twenty minutes and I would feel better, even if just for a day.

One day, I sat in service but a pain in my body became increasingly intense. This was now a distraction. I cannot breathe, and my chest is hurting. Is this how it ends? A heart attack in church? Are you serious? I am not paying for another ambulance ride! I will take an aspirin and it will pass. Yes, that is what I did. It did pass, eventually.

I had now made it a habit to ignore pain. I had even come to expect some level of pain in my body. I knew that my body was reacting to the stressful situation that had become my normal day. So of course, a little pain was going to surface. I am not running back to the doctor. Nothing is different. Yes, I am stressed. Yes, I am obese. No, I am not sleeping. I will be fine – I hoped.

THE POWER OF CONNECTION

During my journey to figure out all the areas of deficiency in my life, I was told that I try to fix everything and never let others help me. Was this a bad thing? I did not want to bother anyone. A person is the sum of the people they hang around. If your inner circle is positive, you will be inspired to be positive. It is the fact of peer pressure. You do not outgrow it. The pressure points change, but they still exist. At this time in my life, I did not want to bring anyone's friend sum into the realm of negativity, lack, depression, or pity. So, I evaded the power of connection. I was doing everyone a favor by staying disconnected. My thought was, "I will eventually figure it out and fix it. Then, I can be useful again."

How do you fix falling apart; mess? Yes, that was a description of me. A falling apart mess of a person. My weight ballooned to reach 70 lbs. of excess me. I was self-conscious, and I found myself crying often. That was a reason I loved to attend church. I could cry in church and no one found this odd. I could let it go and be left alone.

I had a good set of friends that had seen one episode too many of television interventions. No, they did not bring me together as is typically done on the television shows, but they did each have chats with me. I was relieved. I wanted to tell someone that I was hurting, and my love affair was souring rapidly. The great thing about my circle of friends is they never asked the details of what happened. This was important because I was unsure of what was happening. I just knew something was wrong. They simply talked, I listened and cried. I was experiencing my own power of connection. They understood me without me saying a word. And they let me know what they saw.

"This is not normal. You are sick too often. Stress is not your friend and toxic stress will kill you!" Had they been rehearsing the same speech? I heard it repeatedly. To them, the cause of the problem was not as much their concern. The impact on me however, became their point of interest and focus.

MIXED BOWL OF NUTS

While watching television, a commercial appeared that featured Mr. Peanut. Fatigue, emotional decay, and boredom were all at play. I stood up and began to dance and said, "Yes, that is what I feel like. Mr. Peanut. I am living in a mixed bowl of nuts!" I laughed, chuckled, snorted, and then cried. What is happening to me? Where did my joy go? I must get my life back. I must find my love. I hope it is not too late.

I called my mother. I told her of my Mr. Peanut experience. After a moment of silence, she asked, "Do you need me to come to town and be with you?" Although I considered to accept her offer, I replied, "No mom, you do not need to come see me. Save that one-hour plane ride for another day. I am fine."

I was not ok, but I did not want to worry her. I could not explain what was happening to me. I still had not found the words.

Mothers have a special sense about their children. My mom asked, "What ever happened to you starting your own business? Have you done anything with that? It has been a couple of years and I have not heard you say anything about the business."

My initial reaction was to become defensive. Was my mother joining others in pointing out my failures? I started something and did not finish it. Was she also going to help me figure out what was wrong with me?

She noticed my change in energy. She made a statement that hit me hard, "Sweetie there are other jobs out there. It is like a relationship. If it is not working out, go find another!"

Did my mother know? She spoke truth about my situation. My love affair was barely hovering in the zone of like. The relationship was toxic, dysfunctional, and failing miserably. Or was it just me? As the voice in my head replayed the question, 'What is wrong with me?' I began to cry. This cry was different from the daily tears shed after a stressful day. This cry came from the depths of my core. I was in an unhealthy situation mentally, emotionally, and physically. It did not matter how I arrived at this place of toxic stress. It did not matter what I did to try and fix the situation. I was becoming the lady in the restaurant who described waking daily to the agony of being made to go to a work environment that she did not want to be in. I was now the person who joked about my pain and laughed when I wanted to cry. This was not the way love was supposed to feel. I just knew the end was near. My love and I would soon be no more!

My mother patiently listened to me cry and when I settled down she asked, "Would you like to talk about it?" I did. I not only wanted to talk about it. I needed to talk about it! But where do I begin.

"Mom, I love my job. I worked many years to become good at my job. I love my team. We are doing good work. But lately, I do not feel like I fit. I do not agree with multiple decisions. I do not feel like I belong anymore. I am unsure of myself. I am afraid of messing up, constantly. I keep fighting the reality, but this does not feel right anymore. Previously, I would feel anxious when it is time to move locations or change roles. That is not it. It is not about selecting a new city. This is different. I am different. The thing that scares me, is I do not know what I want to do if I do not do this. I do not know who I am anymore. I am stressed, I am unhappy. My body aches with pain and I am entertained by Mr. Peanut. I do not love my job anymore."

I said it. The words fell from my lips as easily as the tears rolled down my cheeks. I do not love my job anymore. Now what?

My mother responded with love and care, "There are plenty of jobs, cities, and opportunities available to you. You simply must choose. Take your time and figure out what is right for you. Do not worry about anyone else. It is time for you to decide by focusing on yourself only. You are not the first person to fall out of love with a job. There is opportunity in change."

She continued, "You often counsel others about workplace issues. It is time to take your own advice. I do not want to receive a call telling me that my daughter had a fade to black moment. You know, that is when something inside is fragile and one more thing can be one thing too many. And your response is excessive and questionable at best. But you have reached your limit so that unsuspecting person will get the pain, hurt, and frustration that has grown inside of you! Let's avoid the fade to black moment. When you are truly tired of being sick and tired, you will make the decisions you need to make. In the meantime, remember how happy you felt when dancing with Mr. Peanut. Take that image with you to work. If nothing, you can enjoy your daily mixed bowl of nuts."

I laughed, "Thank you mom. I am going to be fine, eventually. I really appreciate you." We ended the call and I felt better, clearer, at peace.

My mother is my rock. She accepts me for who I am and does not expect me to always have the answers.

My mother was right. I needed to settle myself and hear the voice inside. I have been guided through times more difficult than this! I decided. These were the last tears of sorrow. I cry no more.

Everyone needs a rock that will lift you higher when the waters of life get too deep. The waters may be high but at least the rock is present for you to stand on and catch your breath.

The next week at work was different. I showed up as a different person. My mindset had changed. I did not have the answers, but I did not fear them either. I was not seeking perfection, but I stopped labeling myself defunct. That lens was no more.

My first indication of change was the detachment from conflict. Previously, I personalized all issues as a failure on my part. This was no longer an acceptable response. I will continue to help solve problems, but they are not all mine. I thought about my mother's advice. I will enjoy my mixed bowl of nuts!

Tuesday morning was a turning point.

Jackson entered my office with a look of panic on his face. I was prepared to help him solve his problem. Let me reiterate-

his problem!

"They are being unreasonable. I do not know what happened. I am not losing my job over this. I refuse. You have to help me," he proclaimed.

He was right. I would help him but not own this problem.

"Mr. Jackson, calm down. What is wrong and what do you need from me to make it right," I asked.

He began to explain, "I have expenses on my credit card. I do not know where they came from. I did not lose my card. I did not let anyone use my card. I searched through all my receipts. I do not know how this happened! I am not losing my job. This is not my fault."

I attempted to calm him, "We will figure this out together. Calm down and let us investigate further. Are you sure the bill is for your card?"

"Yes! The bill matches my card number," he explained.

I asked more questions, "Did you use your card somewhere that you do not normally frequent? Did someone take down your number?"

"No. Nothing new, my card is always in my wallet. I am careful with my card. You must help me. I cannot believe this is happening to me," he shouted.

At this point, he is pacing the floor and visibly upset.

After discussing the matter for an additional fifteen minutes, I still had no idea how this occurred. I will deal with the consequences.

I asked, "Mr. Jackson, what did finance tell you to do?"

As his voice shook from frustration, he says, "They said you need to type a memo stating that you approve the write-off from your department."

I took a deep breath. Last week, I would have been angry

and fearful. I would have found a way to own the mistake. Maybe I did not train him properly. Possibly, did I forget to remind my team to submit receipts? I would have successfully blamed myself for this issue. But not today. That person does not work here anymore.

I replied, "Ok, Mr. Jackson, I will approve the write-off. But know that I need to include a note in your file regarding the circumstance of the write off. We must sit and discuss protocol and ensure this does not happen again. You only get one chance for this error, and you have used your chance. Do I make myself clear?"

He nodded and thanked me.

I opened an email to begin the note. As I addressed the proper finance team member and began to explain the details, I looked at Mr. Jackson who was calming down as time progressed.

I took a deep breath and asked the question that I needed answered to process the request.

"Mr. Jackson, I do not want to lose my job either. We will get through this. How much is the charge-off?"

Mr. Jackson took a deep breath and said, "Three Fifty-Six."

Before I knew it, I was yelling, "Three fifty-six. How in the world do you not know the details of a three-hundred-dollar charge? Are you kidding me? You are going to have to pay it back!"

Mr. Jackson jumps out of his calmly seated position, "Three hundred? Who owes three hundred dollars? I do not have three hundred dollars! My charge is three dollars and fifty-six cents!"

As my ears heard his response and my brain processed this

new-found information, I was not sure if I wanted to hug Mr. Jackson or slap him across the face. I heard my mother's "fade to black rule."

I smiled and said, "Mr. Jackson, we are having this conversation about a $4 charge? We spent the past twenty-five minutes discussing $3.56? Mr. Jackson, I will complete the write-off note, but you owe me a cup of coffee."

He laughed. Then I laughed and said, "Thank you for today's mixed bowl of nuts moment, Mr. Jackson." He looked at me, unsure of what I meant. He smiled, shook his head and walked to the door.

Thank you, Mr. Peanut.

As Mr. Jackson left my office, I realized that it was time for a change. Soon!

A work environment can become so stressful, it causes normal logic to disappear. People are trying to stay out of trouble, not be the one at fault, deflect blame. Everything is a major catastrophe. The concept of opportunity is dead. It is replaced with right and wrong or good and bad. Joyless environments play tricks on your mind. You will find yourself in a mixed bowl of nuts experience!

DRY BONES

While attending a church service, the minister talked about the difference between intellectually understanding a scripture and spiritually living a scripture. He called the latter, the manifestation of scripture in life. I took detailed notes and believed that I understood his explanation. I enjoy thought provoking teaching and learning new concepts.

The weeks at work continued to be difficult but my

response was changed. I was waiting on the answer from my inner voice. I took each day as it came. I found humor in most situations. I even began to smile again. I did not want to make anyone uncomfortable, I just did not want to suffer anymore. It was time to divorce myself from the unhealthy attachment I had to my job. It was time to love me.

I woke one Tuesday morning to a familiar pain in my chest. I had begun seeing a chiropractor and had an appointment that morning, so I decided to discuss the issue with him. He explained that the ongoing spasms had caused a shift in my rib heads. He asked if I had experienced trouble breathing. Of course, I had. He began to ask a series of questions as he felt down my spine. He asked me to sit up. This was different, he had not adjusted me or moved anything around as a visit would normally include.

He looked me straight in the face and said, "Stress will kill you. Your body is doing the best it can, but your lifestyle is not healthy. I will adjust you, but it is not going to get any better if something does not change."

I had heard this before, but this time it sounded different. I heard him say, "Something must change. Are you ready to change?"

I smiled and hugged him. It startled him. He laughed and said, "I have never received that response after my -stress will kill you- speech."

I felt confident in saying, "You are right. It is time for a change. Something has to change, and it will."

I laid back on the table for my adjustment and said, "Fix me up doc. It will be better real soon, I promise."

Later that evening, I attended Bible study at my church. We were discussing the story of Ezekiel and the valley of dry bones. (Ezekiel 37:1-13; NKJV) I had heard the story before.

I was familiar with the scripture. But on this day. I learned. I saw my situation in a different light. I saw myself in the conversation. In the story, Ezekiel is asked by God, if the dry bones could live. Ezekiel responded that God's desire was the answer. God told Ezekiel to speak to the bones and that He, God, would bring the ligaments, skin, and even breath into those once scattered bones. Later in the story, Ezekiel is standing next to the transformed bones, the people identified as the tribe of Israel, after he spoke as commanded by God. The people then shared that they were cut off and hopeless. Ezekiel is commanded to speak again, and the people are restored, placed in their own land, and connected. The people are now aware that it was done to them and for them by God.

I heard the voice inside saying, "Daughter, can these dry bones live? Speak to them and they will."

My work environment had become my valley of dry bones. My job had become my valley of dry bones. My confidence, joy, peace, and love were all represented in the piles of dry bones!

I had the authority to determine if the bones could live, simply by my word. Up until that point, my word had been speaking death into my circumstance. I was not speaking life, breath, or renewal.

I, with confidence replied, "Yes, these dry bones can live! They will live. I will live!"

It was on this day, that I saw my departure from my love, as a gift. A gift to experience life in the valley of dry bones. You see, I realized that my fear of uncertainty and fear of not being in my beloved job was killing me. I was the valley of dry bones. I needed to know that I CAN LIVE. I WILL LIVE outside of these walls. I received a nugget of peace that I held on to daily. I was inspired. I did not know what was next, but

I was less afraid than the day before!

I also realized that my job did not need me. It was fortunate to have me, just as I was fortunate to have it. We would both be just fine.

That was confirmed as we stood at the end of Bible study. I looked around and saw at least 20 people adorned with the company logo. As they stood for final prayer, one by one I realized that my connection to the job opened doors for others to become a part of the family. I opened doors for others just as doors had been opened for me.

This truly was a manifestation experience. The logos that adorned their chests were like the skin covered bones. Ezekiel spoke, and the bones were covered. I too saw covering standing around me. It was a sight that brought tears to my eyes. Tears of joy, peace, and love. The dry bones lived on that Tuesday in Bible study. I smiled.

PEACE IN THE VALLEY

The Bible study experience inspired me. I was reminded that I had value to others. I still had something to give and could benefit those around me. The act of giving was the doorway to my happy space. It was time for me to walk in. My opportunity surfaced within the next few weeks. I remember receiving the phone call asking me to join an assessment team. I had received several requests prior to this date, and my schedule would not allow me to accept the opportunity. But without moving too many appointments around, I felt I could make this one work. Not to mention, the location was exactly what I needed – sunny Arizona. I said yes. I accepted the assignment and looked forward to meeting my fellow assessors in a couple of weeks.

A change in scenery, a new team, and a week in Arizona

was exactly what the doctor ordered. My travel date finally arrived. Arizona in November was a good way to end the Thanksgiving season. I could tell the temperature difference as soon as the plane landed. I looked forward to shedding the winter wear I carried as I headed to the hotel to meet the rest of the team.

Our meeting felt like an All-Star round up. These people were brilliant. I was trying to figure out how I made the line up? Not only were these seasoned professionals, but they were each expert in their field! I felt honored to be allowed to join them and watch the magic. This assignment made me fall in love all over again. To be able to support others in uncovering their opportunity to be the best in class. This was a noble assignment and I was proud to lend my knowledge. As I met with members of the company, I was impressed with their passion and dedication. One person after the other shared amazing stories of accomplishment and a unified desire to do even more.

This is what I was missing. People who were in love with their jobs. People who felt compelled to do more. People like me. It was as if I found my voice again. I was surrounded with others who spoke my language. People who saw the world in a way that I understood. I felt like I had made it home. Each day brought a new adventure. I learned about their plans, hopes, obstacles, and fears. I saw opportunity and promise. I also experienced joy. I was smiling, and no one asked me why.

The trip gave me a different perspective on life. I found peace in the valley of Arizona. This peace had been missing from my life and I did not even realize just how devastating it was for it to be gone. As I helped complete the assessment, I was able to provide hope and perspective to the employees. They wanted to be better. They knew they were good but did not feel like they were prepared to go to the next level. They had all the ingredients. They simply lacked the direction needed to execute the right plan.

On the last night in Arizona, I went out to eat and was taught a valuable lesson. It was sixty-eight degrees and I was wearing a light sweater. As I walked down the Avenue, I passed a lady that was experiencing a very different night air. She had on boots, a lined jacket, hat and scarf. I thought to myself, where could she possibly be going? Why does she have on so many clothes? As we passed, I smiled, and she smiled in return. She looked at me as said, "visiting?" I laughed and responded, "clearly!"

We were walking down the same street on the same night but having very different experiences. I was taking a leisurely warm November stroll while she was hoping the weather did not drop another degree before she made it inside. Neither of us was wrong, we simply had different starting points. My winter low was twenty below zero and her winter low was sixty-eight. The commonality is, everyone gets cold in the winter.

The next morning, I shared my epiphany with the team. Prior to ending the assessment, I told the employees that they were fabulous, and they were on the road to something great. Although they had not arrived, they were not as bad as they believed. I had seen much worse. I thought to myself, "honestly, I was living much worse."

The trip provided me a moment of return. Hope and possibility were returning to my being. I thought to myself, "Do you see what I see? There is a place where I can be me!" This trip alerted me to the need to leave my love and go find me.

JUST STAND UP

As a kid, I never learned to swim. I was terribly afraid of the water. I have a good friend who is as terrified of water as I am. The only difference is, she is substantially taller than me. She stands slightly above six feet tall with no shoes on. Let us just say, my height should not even be discussed in the same context. I have a tall presence, and that is good enough for me.

One day she was at a water park and she decided to try the water slide. She watched multiple patrons slide down and end the wet ride with giggles and joy. For whatever reason, she felt the need to participate and exclaimed, "I want joy and giggles. It is my turn to tackle the slide!" She climbed the stairs and waited patiently as the line progressed on that hot and sunny day. It was about to be her turn. She said she started thinking, "Should I turn back? Wait, am I sure about this?" Although fear set in. She had come too far to turn back. She had to simply take the plunge.

She sat down and with a shove, she was gliding. Too late to think. Too fast to stop. She relaxed and went with the moment. She thought, "This is not that bad. Maybe this is fun? Wait, what happens at the bottom?" She had seen people as they walked away from the pool. But she did not pay attention to the end of the ride. She was uncertain if there was a drop or a lengthy glide. She pondered, "Why did I not figure out how this thing ends!"

Moments later she finds herself terrified and under water. She honestly thought she was going to die. Her emotions were a mixed bag of anger, fear, dread, confusion, and sadness. How did she let this happen?

As she coughed and wailed, she heard a voice in the distance. "What are they saying? Are they talking to me?" She calmed her emotions and focused on the voice. "Stand up. You simply need to stand up." She did not realize that the end of the slide culminated with a glide into a 3-foot splash pool. She was not dying. She did not have to drown. She had to just stand up.

Drowning. That was an accurate description of my existence. My beloved job had become the pool of my demise. The waves were crashing. The chlorine was burning. I could barely catch my breath. My day in the pool was here. Yes, I am terrified of water, and something had to change.

I knew tomorrow would be my last day on the job. I did not know anything else, but THAT fact I was quite certain of. It is over. My love affair has ended. My everything is now a part of my past. Who am I? What do I want? I remember thinking, I have officially hit rock bottom.

The pain I was in did not need to continue. I was not certain where my life was heading. I was unsure of the next steps or the promises of tomorrow. But to end my own suffering, I realized it was time for me to get out of the pool.

A voice inside of me said, "You may be in over your head, but the question is not how deep the water is. The question is, are you standing up while in it." I had to just stand up!

With peace and joy, I walked away. I took that first step into uncertainty. One step at a time, that is how my journey began. I had hit rock bottom and walked into day one of a new journey.

As I caught my breath, I could see the exit. I may be drenched, and a bit worn, but the Tsunami has ended. My fears of uncertainty have been realized. Yes, I have hit rock bottom. There is nowhere to go but up from here, right? Up?

In my darkest moments, I had a guide out of my pain.
Five days earlier I remembered hope and possibility.
This glimmer of light became my Marker of Joy.
There may be signs strategically placed in your life at
this very moment in time. They are present to
encourage you. They demonstrate that you are loved.
They often provide clarity or a different perspective to
consider. Look for markers in your life.

✎ MARKER MESSAGE

At the end of each chapter, is a guided opportunity to reflect on your life and personal circumstances. Pause and examine your own journey. Each Marker Message is placed to evoke a response and inspire actions. I hope my personal Markers of Joy shine light and provide hope to you on your journey.

HITTING ROCK BOTTOM

MARKERS OF JOY

I. Ezekiel was taught your words have power. Speak life into your situation.

To know that my needs will be met brings joy. I rest, and opportunities find me. I arise refreshed and ready for a new day. Resources come easily. No, trouble has not disappeared, but I keep walking forward, fearlessly. I am not alone. I am protected and guided. Others will see my triumph with no effort on my part. In the end all will be well with me. And yes, I will love again! And smile too! (Psalms 23).

Speak power into your life's circumstances and write them down as a reminder of your declaration of power.

II. Is it Me?

You may find yourself looking around and feeling as if you have landed on another planet. Nothing seems to make sense. You thought you understood the rules. You even believed you were a major contributor to the game. But today, you are faced with the reality that something has changed! You are asking, "is it me?" Let me help you, YES, IT IS YOU. You may have reached the point that you are no longer aligned with the status quo. You have

33

✎ MARKER MESSAGE

begun the journey in search of a new normal, because this one is no longer working. Whether it is a relationship, employment, friend group, or book club. If you do not belong and you are trying to understand why no one else sees what you see, you have reached the point of, "so, is it me?" It may be time for you to experience something new. Change is knocking at your door, will you answer? What needs to change in your life? What has been nagging at you? What has been revealed?

III. Your Village Matters.

Hopefully, you have established a healthy circle of support prior to now. This is the group that loves you through the good and the bad. They also have no problem ensuring that you know which of those (good or bad) is happening today. It is not necessary to expose the details of your downward spiral. You do however need to be honest about where you are at this moment. What do you need? What are you feeling? You need to be reminded that YOU HAVE VALUE. So, pack a bag, plan a trip, change scenery even if just for a night. Let those who love you, help you. Your village truly does matter.

Name your village. Who is there for you? Who is in your system of support?

CHAPTER 2
<u>STARTED FROM</u>
<u>THE BOTTOM</u>

*We all have to start from somewhere. There is a peace
and simplicity in new beginnings. Embrace the
opportunity to begin again.*

I have settled into my new existence. Rock Bottom is not my permanent residence, but it is where I reside right now. Like any break up, you begin to unpack the boxes you have accumulated during the relationship. These boxes contain your history of highs and lows. These boxes document the journey. As each box is unpacked, there is the potential to become nostalgic and reminisce about what was. Unfortunately, this reveal can also shed light on matters that had no context while you were living it out. You begin to wonder if you somehow missed the set up? Were there foreshadows ignored? With the opening of each box, my life began to replay before my eyes.

OLD NEWS

As I pulled the tape and listened to the sound of my reveal, I was pleasantly surprised by the first box. This was the box from my rebirth party. Two years earlier, I hosted a birthday party and titled it REBIRTH. Not only was I feeling a need to reinvent myself, but I had also decided to begin my own business. My plan was not fully vetted, but I knew there was a business in me. There were family and friends from near and far in attendance. And yes, my love was present. There were numerous co-workers celebrating my future endeavor. I shared my vision with the crowd. "I want to travel and inspire." I was already known as a trainer and facilitator that can wow a group with a fire-starting speech. My vision seemed reasonable. Create a firestorm of inspiration – that was my new goal.

My first official request came quickly after my announcement. I was contacted to serve as keynote speaker for a college graduation. Is this really happening? They want me to speak? I could not wait to tell everyone at the office. I was not sure what I would speak about, but I knew it was going to be amazing. Amazing for me. I hoped the audience thought so as well. I am on assignment. Let the inspiration begin.

I remember the excitement I felt the morning of the graduation. I was not this excited at my own college graduation. I received my MBA from this institution and did not feel this energized on my commencement day. I was on fire and had prepared to light others ablaze!

Stepping on the stage, I looked around the theatre and realized that I was going to make my debut in front of an audience of more than 2,000 people. Wait, was I ready for this? There was no room for doubt today. Although I had become unsure of myself at work, I knew how to speak to the masses. No time for fear. It was too late now, it was game time!

My name was called, and I rose from my seat. I walked slowly and deliberately to the podium. I smiled and made eye contact with as many of the graduates as I could. I took a deep breath and stepped to the microphone. "Congratulations graduates, you made it. The courses were difficult, and the journey was brutal. You had days that you thought to yourself- this is for the birds. I stand with one simple question. If that is the case- What Kind of Bird Are You?"

I honestly do not remember anything that happened after that moment. I experienced a rush of energy that spoke to me. It lifted me off my feet and allowed me to fly through the air of that monumental moment. I thought to myself, so What Kind of Bird Are You? I was a bird of inspiration. I was a bird of hope. I was a bird of celebration. I was a bird of fire! In that moment of time, I was a phoenix. I just did not realize it yet.

I released my final breath of the keynote fire, and eventually came back to myself. As I became present and grounded again, I was astonished at what happened next. Cheers, clapping hands, yelling voices, and tears greeted me. Amazing. It was amazing for me, and apparently, they experienced amazing as well. I remember thinking, "This is a day I will never forget. This is how I want to feel always. But then there is Monday."

That initial box gave me a different perspective of my past. Was my departure foreshadowed two years before I left? Did I subconsciously begin my exit strategy before I realized I was going anywhere? I am a strategic thinker and planner. But I am not certain that I was psychic as well. My bad days were increasing but my love for my job was very strong. It is possible that I did not want to see what was unfolding before my eyes. I was walking forward with my eyesight jaded by the rose color glasses of love.

As I continued to empty my boxes of old news, more revelations occurred.

I pulled out a picture of my mentor and me.

I remember the confident fire-starter from the graduation remained present for at least two weeks after returning to work. During a coaching session, my mentor commented on the refreshing energy he felt from me. He asked, "What happened? What have you found?" I proudly recounted my experience on stage and how I never wanted that feeling to end. He commented, "It never has to end. That is your purpose. You have been inspiring people for years, but now you are ready for a larger audience."

This concept terrified me! A larger audience? What exactly did he mean? Was I being prepared for something bigger? As the conversation continued, my mentor, Lance, made a statement that foreshadowed my future. "You are going to realize that your assignment is bigger than anything you can imagine. You must keep walking into your destiny. You will know it is time to move when you feel like you are in the wrong place – a place you do not belong."

At the time, I was not ready to hear such a declaration. I even said, "Do not belong? This is my life. How could I not belong to this life?" We ended the session and I tucked the conversation far back in my mind.

As I pulled the final item out of the opened box, I realized, that he was right. My moment of misfit did come.

My mind continued replaying the journey. There were situations that seemed insignificant at the time, but they were glimpses into the future. I looked but somehow did not see.

Your thoughts can be the limiting factor to your future success. Small minds will never be able to dream big!

A KNOCK OUT

As I continued to open boxes it was as if I was taking a walk around the bottom, MY ROCK BOTTOM. Each box revealed the journey down below. I found myself becoming comfortable with the current plateau as I began to comprehend the story of my recent past.

In the next box was a pair of pink boxing gloves and a menu. I remember when my mother came to visit and saw my gloves for the first time. She asked, "when did you start boxing?" I laughed. "I don't actually wear them to box. I keep them as a reminder of my daily battle and the need to be prepared for it."

Did I really say that out loud? As I replay the conversation in my head, I realize how awful that must have sounded to my mom. I am boxing so often, I need a physical reminder to protect myself. She looked at me with tears in her eyes and said, "Baby, I don't know who you are boxing with, but they better not hurt you. I won't let it go 13 rounds. I am a single round type of girl when it comes to my baby! Knock Out – expect it."

I laughed it off and ensured my mom that all was well. That was the story I told her. It was the truth I forced myself to believe. It had to be true, my survival depended on it.

The menu was a tool for my survival as well. When I returned from Arizona, I remember walking in the house yelling, "Honey, I'm home!" I was feeling great and I was on an emotional high. I also realized that I had spent so much time loving my job, I neglected to develop a romantic relationship with any person. I believed that would add complication to my life. I did not have time for the distraction. There were moments I considered giving it a try, but complexities surfaced immediately, and I ran the other way. My empty home neglected to respond. I was home, but there was no honey to welcome me. Late night dinners alone contributed to my desire to eat at restaurants constantly. Although no one was at my table, the establishment had conversations all around, so I did not feel alone. My menu was evidence of my culinary companionship.

My obsession with my job caused me to ignore the months and years passing by as I remained single and married to my career. My grandmother once told me, "Sweetie, you need to focus on your social life. It is not just going to happen. Yes, you are a knock out, but who will know if you never get into the ring?"

My pink boxing gloves were also a reminder of the ring I was not stepping into – the ring of romance. I had convinced myself that I was fine with that as well. Now that my previous love affair was over, I needed to rethink romance. Maybe a change in scenery would help my love life. I needed a new love and I needed to live my life.

For the first time since leaving my job, I became angry and thought to myself, "How many missed opportunities have passed. How many dinners did I decline because it conflicted with the schedule of my beloved job? What was I thinking? Being married to a job does not replace the love of another human being! What have I done?" At that moment, I really wanted to punch something! I refrained. I was in my house and did not plan on replacing any furniture or patching any walls in the coming weeks.

FLY BIRDIE

I have been asked several times, "What was your turning point. You hit rock bottom, but you knew you could not stay there right? How did you work past the pain, anger, and feeling of defeat?"

I respond with a smile, "A little birdie told me it was time."

Unpacking the boxes was slightly therapeutic but I realized that I needed to figure out my next move. The rushing of memories began to send me on an emotional roller coaster that was not healthy.

Initially, I began to panic over the "what ifs."

"What if I don't find another job?"

"What if people are angry with me for leaving them?"

"What if I run out of money and cannot pay my bills?"

Running through a laundry list of what could possibly go wrong is not the same as developing a plan of action. This panic mode has an undertone of defeat. It says that you are worthless, incapable of success, and are a failure.

I truly hope that you have not subscribed to such a narrative about yourself. Trust me, it is easy for that voice to dominate the conversation, especially when fear comes and sits next to you. The two of them can do such a number on your confidence, you may want to run and hide or pray it all goes away. Let me tell you, that does not work either. You are in this for real. Yes, this is happening. Face that truth and get the reality check out of the way! Embrace the bottom. It is not your eternal destination, just a rest stop on your journey. Catch your breath and get ready.

Once I quieted the voice of "what if," another questioner appeared. "So, who do you think you are?" This voice brought shattered self-image, reminders of past failures, and a healthy dose of embarrassment.

I learned to not be afraid of the questioner. It is a necessary path to cross. Knowing who you are will serve as a guide on the journey. Showing up as your authentic self is a responsibility you must prepare for. There is a chance that you have spent significant time being what everyone else needed and expected you to be. Your real self may be tucked so far back in your memory, the question is necessary. Your value is not at question; however, your purpose may be. You have a purpose, but do you know where it fits?

The smartest doctor is not on my call list if the house catches fire! The doctor's brilliance and value are not in question. Having the best person present for the task at hand, is necessary for success.

Back to the question at hand, "Who do I think I am?"

Let me answer that question. I am someone with twenty years of leadership experience. I am someone who has a list of business competencies. I am a team player. I am an inspiration to those I encounter. I am…

What is on your list? So, who do you think you are? Take a moment and answer the question. Write your answer on a piece of paper you can refer to. You may need to carry this script with you to ensure you do not forget.

As I sat in my home with the boxes unpacked and my exploration around rock bottom completed, I looked out the window and saw the most beautiful bird. The bird had a bright yellow breast, red head, and two striped bars on the wing. It was as if the bird had a message for me. It sat on the window ledge and looked me in the eye. Well, I thought it was looking at me.

I decided to google this new visitor and find out the name – Western Tanager. (Field Guide to Birds of North America, n.d.) One of the facts documented about the bird is that it was first recorded on the famous Lewis and Clark expedition. The second fact stated that a group of Tanagers is known as a season of Tanagers.

That was my message! It was time for me to explore. Where would we be if Lewis and Clark had remained in the familiar? What new territories would remain undiscovered had they not ventured out? Lance had been right. It was time for me to expand my territory. Thank you birdie. I hear you, I too am ready to fly. It is my season!

HEALING WATERS

When you have truly decided that success is your destination, you need to declare and believe it for yourself. I called my sounding board, my mom. I needed her to know that I was better. I needed her to know that I was no longer afraid. I was ready to move forward.

An important discovery during your time on the bottom, is uncovering the determination to do something different. Leaving the past behind is more than a box packing exercise. You must go somewhere. So where are you going? You do not have to identify your final destination, just figure out what is next.

I invited my mother to join me for a four-day spa getaway. I had planned and cancelled a trip twice in recent months. It was important for me to do something I enjoyed. I needed to do something for me. It would help me find the clarity needed to develop my plan. I was not cancelling on me this time.

Just thinking about the getaway made me relax.
As my mom and I walked into the front door of the lodge, we were greeted with the smell of pine and the roaring fireplace. The floors were covered with stone slabs that felt like the outside had come in to greet you. The front desk was made of oak and looked rustic and homey. The sound of a waterfall quietly joined the other sensory gifts being presented. The check-in process said, "Welcome home. Come take a load off. We will take it from here."

When becoming free from a stressful environment, it is important to reset your senses. You have trained your mind and body to prepare for battle every day. The morning routine includes putting on the armor and praying to make it through another battle.

When you leave the battle field, your habits do not go away automatically. You must intentionally develop new routines. If Friday was the team meeting that caused your pulse to race, and you have participated every Friday for the past 5 years, guess what happens the first Friday after leaving? Your body will prepare for the adrenaline rush that was previously necessary to make it through the day.

The benefit of such a routine, is you could take up jogging or morning power walks and keep the adrenaline surge going. Or you can create new habits, new ways of being for your system. Whichever you decide, include gratitude in your routine. Remember to be thankful for what did not happen. Be thankful for surviving what did happen. Have gratitude for the adventure to come.

After check-in, we decided to head to the healing pool. This area was adorned with candles, scents like jasmine and eucalyptus in the air. There was a stone whirlpool that included a waterfall. There were recliners surrounding the healing area. People were sleeping, reading, and meditating. As I sat in the pool, the warm healing waters gently massaged every tightened muscle in my body. I was not certain of the exact healing properties, but I felt like a melting stick of butter. I settled into a position on the ledge, laid my head back, and let the warm waves carry my body through a symphony of floating bliss. I was free.

While at the resort, I slept as if comatose. The time of day did not matter. I ate when hunger hit me, and I fell fast asleep again. I was shedding years of stress and strain. There were no alarms or calendars controlling my day. I had a single task on my schedule. Relax. My body was free.

One night, I dreamed of walking through the woods towards a slow-moving stream. I sat next to the water and watched fish swim by, they were orange, yellow, and green. My eyes followed the flight of the butterflies as they landed on the flowers. Roses, orchids, and tulips adorned the plush forest floor. The colors of my dream were vivid. I remember feeling peaceful. The feeling was familiar. I felt creative and alive. The dream was a good one. My mind was finally free.

As the vacation ended, I felt healthier. I was at peace. I was well rested. My mind was clear. I had a spring in my step because joy was flowing on the inside. I was still unsure of my next move, but I was not worried anymore. It was time to go home and see what was next.

TEMPTING OFFER

As I continued finding myself, I began telling others of my availability. I was prepared for my next adventure. It had been two weeks since my departure. That was enough vacation time for me. I was ready to work again.

I received a phone call that made me feel amazing.

"So, I hear you are available now," the voice on the other end was one of my mentors. I smiled. I knew the call would come, but I was not sure when. He continued, "You know I have had a plan for you since the first time we met." I acted as if I was unaware of his plan, "A plan for me?" We both laughed. This was not the first time we covered this topic. He knew that I was fully versed in his plan.

He continued, "There will be an opportunity soon. It has not been announced yet, but I plan to retire, and there needs to be a replacement identified. You know I have always hoped for this to line up. It would be a great opportunity for you. We would be willing to provide transition support and whatever else is needed for you to be successful. You know you can do this!"

I sat on the edge of my seat. It was not so much that my mentor was extending the offer for me to apply to fill his shoes as President/CEO, it was that he trusted me to continue in his footsteps. He trusted me to carry on the legacy of a multi-million-dollar enterprise that encompassed nearly 30 years of his life.

I have seen many movies depicting the passing of the mantle. I was amid my very own mantle moment! I went from feeling defeated and worthless to feeling capable and wanted. I was someone's choice. As he continued to unfold his thoughts about the possibilities, I became excited. I can climb out of the bottom and begin to rise again.

It was as if my turmoil was over. I have been rescued. I thought to myself, "That was not too bad! I was afraid of this? I endured a few weeks of uncertainty. I am ready to go to the predictable future of..." I paused and realized that I may have been someone's choice, but this role was not my choice.

We held a similar conversation six-months earlier. I knew that the possibility existed. If I wanted to assume the role, I had ample opportunity to say yes before now. I found myself sitting with a tempting offer, but not a definite choice.

I had to ask myself, do you want the job or are you running from uncertainty? It was time to be honest with him and myself. That was not the role for me, at least not at that moment.

The work would be pleasantly challenging, the team would be familiar, and the city would feel like home. All those elements were tied with a pretty bow of an impressive salary if I landed the position. However, I could not lie to myself. This was not my dream job. This did not excite me and make me feel like I was walking in purpose. At the time, the role would be a means to an end, but not my desired destination. As honored as I was. As much as I needed to be someone's choice. I had to say no. I was tempted, but I chose no.

When walking around the bottom, the lack of clarity feels like darkness. When you see a glimmer of light, your first inclination is to run to the light. Wait, think, be sure. Your eyes will adjust to the darkness and you will be able to see in ways you never thought possible. Enjoy the glow of the light. Allow it to inform you that you will not be in darkness forever. But allow your eyes to adjust and see through the darkness. Endure the moment. Dark times will come again, but because of this experience, your night vision will be ready!

THE PLAN

The news of my availability spread as if I had a dream team of marketers working on my behalf. I received congratulatory calls, calls of concern, and yes, offers too. It was time for me to decide what I wanted to do. It was time to develop my plan.

I had launched my business. Was that going to be the plan? Inspiration on the road? Although the foundation included inspiration, there was more. I was not quite sure of the details, but I knew they would reveal themselves soon.

As I continued to examine what I did not want to do, I needed to gain clarity on my desired opportunities.

I reflected on the assessment assignment. My experience in Arizona was a positive one. I made a phone call to the company in Arizona. Maybe they knew of other opportunities in the region. My call was received with excitement. I shared my plan and asked for referrals. To my delight, they were aware of an immediate opportunity. A local organization had a recent assessment completed and they were beginning to address the areas of need highlighted in the report.

I was surprised and excited. What great timing. I wondered what sort of support was needed. I was willing to submit a proposal and meet with the decision makers to make this opportunity a reality. The next piece of information was the best news I had heard in quite a while.

I pulled out my notebook and prepared to write the contact information for the company that I was going to approach. I was excited to present my credentials and work history to the company's leader. I asked, "How well do you know the decision maker of this group that needs support?" As I heard laughter coming from the other end of the call, I was confused. Had I missed a joke? The irony quickly became clear as she explained more. The decision maker, the company that needed help, was the person I had called. I remember thinking, "wait, what?" She said with a chuckle in her voice, "Yes, you heard me right. We need you. When can you get here? We have a meeting next week; can you make it?"

Because of my shock, I stumbled on my words, "Next week... no.... I... wait..." I was baffled, this was happening so fast. I was not prepared for this conversation. I gained my composure and answered, "No I cannot come for a few weeks, but can we spend that time ironing out the details?" She agreed, and my first official solo contract was born. I am open for business.

THE GREAT RETURN

After walking around in emotional darkness for 30 days, it was time to embrace sunshine. As I boarded the airplane for

Arizona, I remembered hearing a random fact – the sun shines 85% of the year in Phoenix. Considering the eclipse I experienced, I was ready for sun and more sun. Arizona, here I come. I was now on journey day thirty-one. It was officially one month since hitting rock bottom.

I completed the assessment and left my job exactly 30 days prior to my return to the dessert. So much had occurred in such a short period of time. I looked forward to my wilderness adventure. I felt like I was experiencing the story of Jeremiah in the Bible. God informed Jeremiah that He appointed him for a specific role. (Jeremiah 1:5-7; NIV)

It is said that a specific plan was created for each person prior to their birth (Jeremiah 29:11; NIV) Life experiences occur to prepare a person to fulfill his or her plan. Everything you need has been predestined. You simply need to put in the work to experience the adventure of the journey. Jeremiah was assigned to bring a message. The message was made for that specific moment in time. I believed this was my time. I had over twenty years of experience and the company had a need for my expertise.

When experiencing the downward spiral towards the bottom, you forget previous wins. You forget the challenges you have overcome. You even forget what you are capable of accomplishing. But then an assignment comes your way, tailormade for you. It is at that moment, you regain your identity. You remember your old self. If you are fortunate, you step up to the challenge, and show what you are made of!

My return to Arizona was joyful. You see, I had fond memories of the area. My grandparents had a home in Arizona when I was a teenager. I remember sitting by the pool, watching my cousins play in the water. I remember taking walks to the movie theater. My grandma would tell us to come in out of the sun, but for some reason, I never got too hot. I loved the feel of the warmth on my skin. I marveled at the beauty around. To see the pink hue of a flower growing out the cactus fascinated me. The cactus was thick and spiked. It looked rough and scary, but there was the contrast of the vibrant flower showing in all its glory. It drew you in. It almost did not look real. That was the perfect metaphor of my life. It was thorny, rough, and scary, but I knew beauty was about to bud. Beauty so amazing that you could not take your eye off it!

When I visited my grandparents, I felt free and at peace. I always told myself that I would retire and return to Arizona to live. I was in my happy place starting my next phase of life. The plan for my life and its components were lining up. Being placed on the assessment team was no coincidence. It was a step on the path to my next adventure. I was not aware, but I am so glad I said yes! It was as if I was experiencing a foreshadow of things to come. A glimpse of what was possible. Like the cactus plant, I was in a place that was made for me and me for it. I was ready to grow and begin my official bloom!

There comes a point when you must take steps forward, into your new. It may be scary, and you will not have all the answers. One step, one day, one decision at a time. Standing still is not an option. As you figure things out, begin with what you know. Start with the familiar. Who can you call? Which path can you explore? The voice inside will guide you, be prepared to listen.

GAME ON

The leader of the company, Lisa, was brilliant. She was a bundle of energy that swept through a room like the

Tasmanian devil. She had high expectations and worked very hard for what she wanted. Her outlook on life was not only positive. She believed everything was possible! She inspired me to be better. She excited me to work hard. Her rallying cry was, "Game on!" She expected everyone to bring their 'A Game,' to the situation. She also wanted everyone to enjoy the experience. She had a positive outlook at the game of life and it was contagious! She was the type of leader I would follow to the end. I was proud to help in every way that I could.

As I understood the goals and wrapped my mind around the task, I became inspired. I could do this. I would do this. I was made for this assignment. The company had several divisions that, over time, began functioning as independent firms. The differences moved beyond regional specialties. There was a lack of alignment that made the business function in a disjointed manner. The need for oneness was apparent.

The challenge was to allow everyone to maintain their unique perspectives and not rob any location of its individuality, but systems had to be developed. The experience for the customer should be the same, regardless of which address they frequented. High quality and the experience of excellence must be consistent across the enterprise.

As I worked with the team, I realized that I began to care. Not only was I concerned about their work, I had the opportunity to see the talents and gifts each person brought to the table. There were opportunities to make changes, but I was hesitant to move too fast. As a seasoned leader, I knew the appropriate cycle of evaluation, information, communication, planning, and action. But I was not comfortable moving forward with my ideas. My confidence had not been restored. I refused to mess up. One day, while in conversation with Lisa, I shared my ideas and concepts. She looked and stated, "I was wondering what you were waiting on. Move already. Game on!"

The conversation lit a flame. I heard the starter's pistol. I saw the green light. I heard the whistle blow. Game on! The runner that hesitates to leave the starter block loses ground and must work harder to make up the distance caused by the delay. I wanted to run the race. I wanted to win. After receiving the green light from Lisa, I was ready. I brought the team together and shared my plans. The conversation was magical. There were ideas, laughter, and individuals volunteering to lead components of the plan. I was pleasantly surprised. I then remembered the energy of my visit a month prior. This team wanted to win. They hoped for better and were committed to making better happen. When I went home that night, I reflected on the success of the day. I promised myself from that moment forward, I would take a chance, they did. They took a chance on me! I would no longer hesitate. I would be present and give my best without holding back. I was in place to flourish.

Gandhi said, "Be the change you want to see in the world." (Quotable Quotes. n.d.) The next part of my plan was to encourage everyone to be conscious of their personal health. When a team is filled with overachievers, dedicated, focused members, the leader may need to remind them to take care of self. It was time for me to change my life. My health had been ignored for too long. Valentine's day was approaching, and I decided that I would choose to love me by being healthier. If I wanted to enjoy this new freedom, I needed to focus on a healthier me. I shared my "healthier me" concept with the team. I told them it is time for me to LIVE LOVE. I could no longer simply exist. It was time to live my life and love every moment of it. The team agreed to join me in the effort. Each person identified how they would LIVE LOVE. We became focused on better for ourselves as we provided better for those we served. Some team members chose to eliminate habits from their life. Others decided it was time to return to past hobbies or begin something new. I needed to focus on my mental and physical well-being. I even had a LIVE LOVE t-shirt made so I could be reminded of my promise.

I was introduced to the concept of thoughtfulness walks. The idea is to allow your mind to shed all negative thoughts and clutter as you take walks. It allows you to see your environment. You become present to things around you. As I became committed to my daily walks, I noticed flowers and birds. I saw beautiful homes and breathtaking skies. The mountains spoke to me. They encouraged me to fear no obstacle; to pursue what I wanted and speak my truth. I was one with nature and it was healing me.

I felt more confident. I was smiling again. And I let others know that I cared. I had high expectations, but I believed the goals were possible. I found a safe place to be me.

CRACKED

When recovering from a bad break-up, there is always the chance for a flashback. You believe you have moved on. You are sure that your heart has healed. Then something occurs that makes you realize, there is still room for growth.

The day began as pleasant as every other day had been. I was working on a project and focused on meeting a deadline. I needed information from several departments and had communicated the urgency of my request. No one came with questions, so I hoped they were moving forward on my request. A member of the department I requested information from, walked by my desk as he headed into a colleague's office.

For some strange reason, I became uneasy. Was my request unrealistic? Did I offend them by asking for so much information? Were they in the office discussing me at that very moment? As the minutes passed, I began to panic. Had I upset our harmonious environment? What should I do to fix it?

I rose from my desk and walked slowly down the hall. I rehearsed my apology as I walked towards the office. I still needed the information, but I did not need anyone upset with me. I braced myself and prepared to walk in to the room knowing I was the subject of conversation. You know how that feels. Everyone stops talking and tries to appear normal, but the tension is undeniable.

I took a deep breath and prepared to knock on the door. Before my hand made contact, my colleague opened the door and grabbed my hand, "Come in, I was just coming to get you. You have to see this video, it is hilarious."

I was confused. I thought, "A video? They are huddled in the office because of a video?" They both had tears in their eyes as if they were crying. On the screen was a video where they inserted their faces on two dancing characters. They wanted to send this video out to the rest of the team. They thought it would brighten everyone's day.

I realized that I had overreacted. My teammates were enjoying a moment of joy. They were sticking to their commitment to LIVE LOVE. A daily laugh break was on their schedule. The video was hilarious. The story I created however, was no laughing matter.

I saw myself and was ashamed. Picture this, you are walking around with an arm full of eggs. Not the pretty, decorated, boiled eggs the children have at Easter. No, an arm full of fragile, raw, fresh eggs. Each egg represents a past hurt, a trauma, a fear. You carry this bundle daily. You never put it down. No matter how tired your arms may be, you always have your eggs. Imagine what functioning must be like. You see a coworker who greets you with a smile and waves excitedly. You can't wave back with the same enthusiasm because you may drop an egg. The horrible mess it will make. No, you can't let that happen. Later in the day, you are in a team meeting and everyone is asked to have all hands-on deck. Hands on? Your arms are full. You don't have a free hand to help others. You need help with your arms full of eggs. Someone may notice that you are not engaged. They are concerned so their response is to lean in and provide comfort, but you push them away. If anyone gets too close, they will crush your eggs. The eggs will be a smashed, dripping, mess all over you. No, do not let anyone too close. You must protect your eggs.

Although this analogy may sound ridiculous, this is what happens when we are not fully healed from hurt. Our burdens interfere with our ability to move on. It interrupts our attempt to step forward. Can you imagine trying to jump for joy with an arm full of eggs. Well that is what happens. We have a moment of joy, but the voice inside quickly reminds us of the beloved eggs. Are you thinking about choosing joy over your pain? Are you ignoring what happened? You must not crack that egg!

I urge you to toss the eggs. Stop carrying around those burdens that have stifled you for so long!

I realized that my eggs were cracking. I thought my colleagues were discussing the mess of egg on my face, but only I could see the egg. Only I knew of my pain. I walked in the office prepared to defend my sacred eggs, but I walked into a room so full of joy that I refused to stink it up with my eggs. On that day, I chose joy.

I thanked them for sharing their funny times with me. I

left the office feeling like a fool. I created a story in my head based upon what? I was not paranoid, I was traumatized. I had spent time experiencing closed doors, blindsides, back stabbing, conflict creating, miserable work days. I thought it was over, but I had brought the pain with me. I still carried sensitivities from past hurt. I packed my eggs instead of leaving them behind. The healing process was not yet complete.

I learned a valuable lesson on this day. Be aware of your personal baggage. Make sure you unpack your baggage and discard the container, as to not fill it again. I am in a new place. It is time for me to act like it. I needed to let the past pass! I will no longer carry the stench of those eggs in my life. That has come to an end!

I left for lunch and to get some air. When I returned there was an email with every item I requested for the project deadline, and additional suggestions to improve the final product. Included in the email was a note of gratitude:

"Thank you for what you bring out of us. Your faith in us is inspiring. It is a pleasure to work with you. If you need anything else, please do not hesitate to ask. We Got This!"

I was concerned that my request for support angered someone; in reality, they were being stretched and inspired. I was so grateful for this experience. I was learning to believe again. We Got This – indeed! The previous silos were disappearing, and the team was growing closer. The strategic changes were taking place and the organization's foundation was solid. They were ready to build, grow, and excel.

SOLID FOUNDATION

I had been in Arizona for several months now. We agreed that this would be a six-month contract. My confidence grew daily as I experienced challenges and uncovered areas to better align the company. I noticed people continuing their joy journeys. More importantly, I saw people experiencing joy together. The bonding I witnessed was beautiful. I was also benefitting from the environment of joy. I too felt as if my foundation was solidifying. My new company's purpose was clear, and my skills were being used. I even found personal time to experience the beauty of Arizona.

As I continued my daily walks, I took pictures of flowers, birds, and mountain views. I wanted to capture the beauty of my surroundings. My walks were my LIVE LOVE commitment. I had no problem rising early in the morning and walking with the early morning sun. I often passed others walking early as well. It was later explained to me that in the heat of summer, it is too hot to walk later in the morning. That explained a lot. I thought it was odd for there to be so much movement at 6 am, but I get it now. My walking was no longer an office challenge fulfilled or a quick fix fitness stunt, I loved and looked forward to my morning walks. I am not sure why I had never considered this activity before, but I knew this was going to be a permanent habit in my life.

I was aware of the benefits of daily exercise, but it always seemed like such a chore. This, however was enjoyable. It was peaceful, joyful, and freeing. When I walked, my mind was creatively flowing with ideas. I found myself laughing, sometimes for no reason at all. The joy was so extreme and flowed so freely. I was experiencing bliss!

On one of my walks, I stopped to take a photo of a beautiful cactus garden in front of a home I passed. The garden spoke to me. It inspired me. Instead of taking a picture of the garden, I took a selfie. I joined in the shot with my new-found friends. I was smiling as the thorns adorned my space.

I sent the photo to my mom and she called me

immediately. I thought she was calling about the beauty of the plants I captured. "Hey mom, aren't they gorgeous?" She laughed and said, "They are gorgeous, but you are glowing. The desert agrees with you! You look amazing."

Let's be clear, moms are usually the ones to believe the best of their children and are willing to celebrate the smallest victory. I love my mom and she loves me. I replied, "Thank you mom. I feel amazing. I guess you can see me LIVE LOVE." She replied enthusiastically, "Yes I can. You look healthy, happy, and smaller. Have you lost weight?"

In the past, that question may have hurt because the answer was clearly NO. Today this was a question that made me smile. I replied, "I have lost weight mom. I'm not sure how much, but my clothing size has gone down. That's a good sign." I was not focused on losing weight. I was focused on my fight to LIVE LOVE.

I had dropped nearly six sizes in clothing. All that had been eating me, was gone. I guess I simply walked it off. My daily strolls renewed my mind and freed my soul. My mind and body were unrestricted. Those walks apparently were burning calories as well.

I did not realize how fulfilling it could be to develop an active lifestyle. At the end of a rough day, you can simply sweat it off. To begin a new day, you can walk into your joy. I was hooked on this new lifestyle. A solid foundation was being laid for a healthier me! I also added Zumba to the regimen. My love for music was being fulfilled as I burned calories. My life's soundtrack was turned up to 10 and it sounded sweet to me.

I continued to take pictures during my daily walks and my joy was overflowing. I began sharing daily pictures and words of encouragement. I was determined to spread joy, hope, and love. I simply wanted everyone to feel as amazing as I did.

MINDSET

As I continued to see positive developments within the company, I also noticed changes within myself. My mindset had changed. I was no longer trying to forget what happened in my past. The ache had finally stopped. I remember the moment vividly. I was completing my walk and I sent an inspirational message. The message was my indication that I was finally better:

Thorny places - March 11th. Sometimes life can seem prickly, like more than you can bare. But look closer. It's all for your good! The thorns are there to ensure you don't get complacent. Keep moving forward. In that thorny place is rare beauty, placed there so you don't lose hope. It's placed there just for YOU!

After I sent the message, a feeling of relief came over me. I began to weep. This was not like my previous moments of breakdown. This cry was like the first breath taken by a newborn baby. This cry was the announcement of my presence. I cried for joy. I cried all the hurt out of my heart. I was ready for the pain to end. I stood in a pool of tears on day 93 of my journey. I was a kid dancing in the puddle. My puddle of joy was created by my tears, evoked by my understanding of thorny places.

As I walked back to my home, I tried to remember when the pain subsided. How many days or weeks had it been since I agonized over my lost love? I honestly could not recall, and it did not matter. I was in love again. I was head over heels in love with me!

After hitting Rock Bottom and beginning to start over, there is the necessary step of ensuring you are there for you. Self-neglect, undue stress, and bad habits must not continue with you on your journey upward. You cannot heal a broken limb by continuing the behavior that broke it to begin with. Take a pause and let things mend. Then you can revisit past behaviors appropriately, having learned your lesson and eyes wide open.

THE REFRAME

My new mindset not only impacted my view of the past, it gave me a different lens in which to experience the present. I had reframed every aspect of my life. While in a meeting, I joked about my love for opportunities. My comment was laced with a little bit of sarcasm. Someone in the room said, "You know what, I have enjoyed our latest challenges. We have worked together and solved problems I never realized we could overcome." Another team member chimed in, "And I have had fun doing it too." I smiled and said, "See I told you, I love opportunities!" This time, there was no sarcasm. It was as if we all realized that together we were unstoppable! From that moment forward, I faced challenges as the opportunities they truly were. I was no longer self-conscious and unsure. I was confident and embraced opportunities.

There may be an opportunity for increased communication across the team. There is opportunity for someone to learn a new skill. There is an opportunity to learn from our mistakes. And there is an opportunity to do it better today, then yesterday. I will never rob myself or those around me, of the joy of opportunity.

As the alignment continued to emerge and opportunities were embraced, the temperature rose as well. I recalled my childhood walks in the sun and realized that my now adult body was not prepared for the heat. Two bouts with dehydration is what really taught me the lesson. Nonetheless, I still enjoyed the desert life. I found my paradise. I just had to remember to bring my own water!

My goal was to now ensure that the entire company found their joy. I wanted everyone to continue to LIVE LOVE, but also to spread joy like a wildfire. We therefore decided to initiate an internal campaign called "212 Degrees." We were excited about the concept and had heard of its success at other companies. Now it was our turn! A team of ambassadors were gathered, and the planning began. The concept was based upon the book by Sam Parker & Mac Anderson entitled 212- The Extra Degree. The book focuses on the need to take 'it' a step further. You decide your 'it,' but to achieve success requires more than normal.

The team was excited as we embraced this company-wide initiative. We were committed to go a little further than any of us had ever been before. It was hard, uncertain, and amazing.

YEAR OF FAVOR

While working in Arizona I was introduced to a local church that became my place of worship. The Pastor declared, "This is THE YEAR OF FAVOR!" He challenged everyone to expect things to work out for them. He told us to demand positive things to occur in our lives and walk in the confidence of winners. The message resonated with me. I believed that I was living in a season of favor. I expected amazing. No matter what it looked like, I knew to remain calm because in the end,

I win.

This concept is not one that is easily understood. We focus on our circumstance and try to figure out how we can fix it. When we do not uncover a solution, we consider it failure. I have learned that there are some situations that are not supposed to work out as you expected because four steps down the road something else is waiting. I learned to not be anxious. I put my trust in a higher authority and rest with confidence.

The church had an amazing choir. The group was talented and had beautiful voices. More importantly, they had a presence and energy that was contagious, uplifting, heartfelt, and pure. It was through this group that my soundtrack of favor was developed.

One Sunday, they sang a song entitled, "Everlasting God." (Murphy, W. 2016). I attended church regularly and I had what I considered a healthy spiritual life. I prayed, read the bible, and believed in the relationship principles of my holy covenant. But when I paid attention to the lyrics of this song for the first time, I was floored. It was saying everything I felt but had not taken time to say out loud. It spoke my truth:

"The Lord is my light and Salvation! Whom shall I fear? Whom shall I be afraid? I will wait for you! I will remain confident in this, I will see the goodness of the Lord!"

As the lyrics of the song danced on my heart, I had an epiphany. I realized that I was no longer fearful of uncertainty. I looked forward to newness. I embraced growth and opportunity. I was not in control and I did not want to be either. I had spent six months on my first contract under my personal brand and I loved every moment of it. I had not planned this move. I walked through the doors of opportunity and it worked out for my good. That made perfect sense to me.

After all, this was the Year of Favor!

ALIGNED

As I worked with the company on the alignment, my business structure became clear to me. In the beginning, I envisioned traveling and speaking to audiences about empowerment and inspiration. That vision was too shallow. The dept of the plan had not yet been revealed to me. Through the alignment process, my model took form. I was clear of the deliverables for my client. These actions were fundamental to moving the company forward.

Ironically, I had been a consultant for 15 years, for someone else, but never thought about those tasks as key components to my new journey. Everything I needed had already been provided. I simply needed to put the tools to work. Once again, I was reminded of who I was and what I can do.

During the final days of my contract, staff began to provide me with feedback on the 6-month journey we were completing. One conversation touched me as it summed up the experience for us all. One member of the team said, "You know what we call you?" I was afraid to hear the answer to that question, but I pursued. I replied, "Do I want to know?" She laughed and said, "It is not as bad as you may think. We call you Mary Poppins. You have mastered the spoon full of sugar approach." I laughed and replied, "That is an accurate depiction of my mindset. It does take a spoon full of sugar to make the medicine go down! As unpleasant as the taste may be, the cure is worth the discomfort."

The assignment was successful because it was personal. I wanted to do well for my client. No, I needed to do well for my client. I needed to do well for me.

As I built relationships with the staff, I wanted to give them what they needed to be successful. I wanted them to have all the tools and resources to do well. This required both of us to put in the work.

They had to be prepared to be stretched. As we moved beyond the normal, I was stretching their thought process and challenging the status quo. There were days where I felt I was pushing the big rock up the steep mountainside. Once trust was built, we were pushing the rock together. There were also periods of pull. They saw the vision and knew victory was on the other side, but the journey between here and there, included crossing the bridge of uncertainty. We had to establish confidence in each person. It was important for them to realize they had what was necessary to be successful on the other side. They each wondered, "Will my skills be enough for tomorrow's requirements? If not, is there a safe space for me to ask for help?" The answer to all concerns was – Yes!

Finally, I had to help them heal. I was willing to apologize for the past wrongs and acknowledge that some things simply were not right. Once we worked together to lay a solid foundation and build a healthy culture, it was time for me to leave. Just as Mary Poppins, the winds of change have arrived, so I must go.

I could not be selfish. I had to hand off this amazing team to their new leader. I was the builder who loved every moment from the laying of cement to putting out the welcome mat. As the beautiful new house, built by love, stood ready to be occupied, I needed to accept that this was not my home. My work was coming to an end. It was time to hand over the keys.

Everything aligned! The timing was perfect. I was approaching what would have been my 20th anniversary with one company. Instead I was celebrating year one of a new journey, made possible by 19 years of intense preparation. I was in a great place in my life.

SERVE OTHERS

While in Arizona, I also continued working with groups back home in Wisconsin. I began group coaching sessions. I enjoyed the group coaching because it allowed me to feel connected to home. Although, I was happy to be away, I felt a little guilty too. I left the city abruptly and began my new endeavor. Someone asked why I did not find a local contract instead of leaving town. I needed such a drastic change in my life, relocation was a necessary strategy for me. And once I arrived, I wanted it to never end. I did however feel guilty about those I left behind. Coaching allowed me to stay engaged in the community and not totally abandon the needs that existed there. And technology made it possible to have the best of both worlds.

A consistent joke during my coaching calls was the inquiry about the weather. Someone would say, "so how is the weather?" I would respond, "not as good as it could be." We would laugh because everyone knew that I was sitting on the deck in the sun in the middle of March, enjoying the Arizona winter.

My coaching allowed me to provide support in the development of business skills, as well as a listening ear. This project focused on church alignment. My group consisted of leaders. They were all responsible for segments of the ministry and faced moments of frustration, disappointment, and a desire to flee. I knew this feeling all too well. I felt honored serving as their guide to a better future.

One member of the team was a person that I knew as an acquaintance but during this process we became friends. I am not sure how it happened, but he was a special task for me. Let's call him Clark. Our coaching began with me challenging his disposition. He seemed disconnected, unconcerned, and unhappy most of the time. During a one-on-one call, I asked him for feedback on my perception of his disposition. He hesitated but then began to explain. He agreed with my perception, but he stated that the external did not match his heart. Inside, he wanted joy, had ideas, and did not want to be stuck. I was pleased to know that he wanted something different. Initially, I was worried that my efforts were useless because his wall was so intense. I learned, the wall was a defense and he stood on the other side hoping for someone to ask to come in.

As our friendship developed our trust grew. He even asked that I share advice related to his personal life. He sometimes asked for a female perspective on decisions. I was glad to listen and counsel. It allowed me to take my mind off my life. Our conversations were entertaining as well. It is amazing how differently men and women experience matters. But that is a totally different topic! During one conversation he remarked that he appreciated that I understood him. He said he felt comfortable talking to me and did not feel judged.

He was very interesting to me. His life read like a made for television movie. There were good times, bad times, and craziness in between. I felt humbled that he trusted me with his secrets, fears, and moments of vulnerability. There was nothing for me to judge. I was there to help forge a new beginning. His past was an ingredient to his make-up. In that moment, it was not right or wrong, it was simply him. It was Clark.

We had several interests in common which gave us topics to discuss in between counseling sessions. He appreciated and understood that my life had a soundtrack. He loved music as much as me. We also both shared a love for the southwest. I planned to make Arizona my home and he had set his mind on Texas, although he had considered Arizona at one point in time.

His knowledge of Texas came in handy. I was scheduled to attend a conference there within the week and needed advice on social opportunities while in town. He agreed to serve as my concierge on call. During my visit, I texted him to share my enlightenment regarding the beauty Texas had to offer. The conference allowed one night of freedom. I knew who to contact. I texted him to find out where we should explore. Instead of responding he called.

"Did you call me," he asked. I had texted but not called. "No, I did not call. I texted you. Did my phone dial you," I responded. He laughed and said, "You do not have to make up excuses to call me. You can just call."

I remember laughing and wondering if he was flirting with me? I responded, "If I wanted to call, I would. I am not afraid of you. Remember, I saw behind that wall already!"

We both laughed, and he gave me the information I requested. I was less interested in the potential flirting, than I was inspired that he was willing to play! It warmed my heart. That exchange reminded me of a turning point for the character in Disney's Beauty & the Beast. The character "Beast" was introduced as a savage, angry, aggressive, horrifying beast that was cold-hearted and to be feared and left alone. As the movie progresses, you find out that he had endured heart ache, pain, and a curse. His heart was broken, and the beast persona was protecting what was left of his fragile existence. He wanted to love but had grown comfortable pushing others away because it hurt less than rejection. This was Clark. He was softening. He was trusting. He was not as scary as I first secretly perceived. He was coming around. His exterior was beginning to match his heart. He even smiled.

The week before I moved back to Wisconsin, from Arizona, Clark called me to share exciting news. He was moving south. He had accepted a job in Texas and was relocating at the end of the week. I was very happy for him. I was happy for his chance to move to a place he loved, as well as happy to hear that he was going to take a chance at love. He had a friend that had been an on again, off again component of his life. They were going to see what was possible. Over time, I had become very fond of him. I felt like he was a good guy and deserved happiness. I congratulated him on his new adventure and told him that I was there if he ever needed me. I was proud to have played a role in helping someone LIVE LOVE.

SHE REIGNS

Before leaving Arizona, I had the opportunity to attend a women's conference. The conference was titled "She Reigns." The focus was understanding your role and authority as a queen. Women lead companies, households, and communities. There often comes the time when a woman's crown is off-centered, and she needs to be reminded of who she is. The conference was attended by hundreds of women from around the country. The diversity was beautiful, and the energy was magnetic! I did not want to miss a thing.

I was scheduled to return home to Milwaukee after the conference and I wanted my desert experience to last. During one of the sessions, a message was delivered that forever changed my life. It was as if my final step of leaving the past hurt was being achieved through this conference. Pastor Sheryl Brady addressed the delegation. She was powerful and direct. Her message was clear, and her passion was incredible to witness. During her address, she made the statement that completed my process.

She said, "Ladies as you exit the storm you were in, you will be better. You will not only have survived, you will thrive. But before you go forward celebrating your new-found freedom, take a moment and forgive the process."

Forgive the Process. Those words took me through a portal of consciousness that I had never experienced before. I instantly saw the faces, heard the voices, felt the pain caused by those involved in my past. It was as if I climbed aboard a rollercoaster that sped through a museum of my life. What was happening to me? Where did all this come from?

When I mentally returned to the sanctuary, Sheryl was praying, and I was crying. I understood in the depths of my soul, that I was not allowed to rejoice in my new life without first acknowledging that others played the necessary roles assigned to them. They were key actors in the script that led to my current state of bliss! Not only should I forgive them, I should be grateful for the difficult tasks placed on their heads. Wow! That is why you can love your enemy.

That was the final step. I was not angry nor was I in pain, but I had not released them from blame. I had not forgiven. At that moment, I was set free from every piece of residue that had hung around from back when. I was liberated. Now I will LIVE LOVE indeed.

> When you do not forgive, you are not free. As you hold the person in the stockade of your unforgiveness, you must stand guard to ensure they do not break free! Forgiveness is for you, before it has any impact on them.

The final message of the conference focused on healing. "Woman you are healed." I had accepted my healing prior to this message, however I felt a knot in the pit of my stomach. I interpreted it to mean, "Woman stay healed."

I left my desert paradise and returned home to Milwaukee. I was not sure what was next, but I was ready. I had a business model, I loved me, and I was open to the journey down the path of uncertainty. When I landed the next day, I posted a message to the world, "She is back!" My home front had not changed, but as for me, nothing was the same.

I spent the next week making plans. I decided that it was time to move. I was moving to Arizona. I did not have to wait until retirement. That could be my home right now. I was determined to return to my paradise as soon as possible. Although I started the year at the bottom, I was ready to climb to a new height.

ON ASSIGNMENT

As a leader, I felt lonely. I had moments of insecurity. I even lacked confidence at times. Leadership is difficult. Leaders need support too. I was clear that my purpose had been revealed. For my entire adult life, I worked as the co-pilot for amazing leaders. I loved to serve. I loved to help prepare them to walk into battle and win. I had intuition, experience, and a track record of strategic thought and creativity. I was a strategist who loved to sit next to the leader and help make amazing happen. That was my life's purpose and I was moving to Arizona to roll up my sleeves and serve. It was time to return to Milwaukee and continue to climb out of the bottom that had been my dwelling place. My assignment had come to an end and I returned home.

I contacted my closest friends and updated them on my relocation plan. They were proud and more than willing to help me pack my life away, so the journey could begin. Another supporter asked me to showcase my new brand at her upcoming empowerment brunch. I was honored and agreed to do so. Her brunch was a community event that had developed a faithful following of go-getters. Guest speakers, vendors, and honorees were a part of the program, and I was going to be present.

I was focused on my relocation efforts. I spent the next week packing away items I did not need for daily life. This task required a committee of friends. I needed their guidance and muscle to purge. I was not a hoarder, but pack-rat was a fitting title. They knew this about me and had no problem letting me know it.

On the upcoming Saturday, I was showcasing my company. I had two components to my business solution. The first focused on the leadership of the company. This component was branded – LEADERS LEAD. The second component of the strategy focused on the team and was inspired by my experience in paradise, and it was branded – LIVE LOVE. I had a busy week, but Saturday was going to be exciting.

A few weeks earlier, as I prepared to leave Arizona, I made several appointments that would occur as soon as I returned home. I did not think the plan through. The result was five days of scrambling to various parts of the city because I planned an over active calendar. What was I thinking? The one appointment I looked forward to attending was my annual doctor's visit. I had lost nearly 50 pounds. He was going to be floored. I had not felt this good since college. I could not wait to brag.

I had been posting messages on social media, but decided I wanted to create an official blog. So, my official #LIVELOVE blog was born. I wanted to help others enjoy the life they lived. I posted my inaugural message to launch on Saturday while I premiered my brand at the brunch:

Live Love is a Movement inspired by the goal to get the most out of the single, irreplaceable life you have been given! We spend endless days, months, years, BEING – but we often forget what happened or how we felt. That's because we are called to LIVE, not just be. That requires presence, intentionality and purpose! Secondly, we tolerate, survive, and sleepwalk through our life. That's not good enough. You were called to LOVE. So, join the LIVE LOVE Movement! Commit to LIVE LOVE. Post how you chose to LIVE LOVE today and convince others to do the same. #LIVELOVE. Together, we will make this world a better place.

I hoped to introduce people to the message at the event on Saturday. I said to myself, "I am going to show everyone how to LIVE LOVE. #LIVELOVE is me!"

Friday had arrived, and I was one day from the event. My business reveal was less than 24 hours away.

I remembered that my doctor was supposed to call me regarding my test results. He said something needed to be run again. I carried my phone as I packed my car in preparation for tomorrow's event. The phone rang as I was loading the trunk.

I answered the phone, "Hello doctor, how are you? Now is a good time. Yes, I can talk. Let me go back into the house so I can hear better."

"What did you just say?" I was uncertain if I was hearing the doctor correctly! The room spun, and I gripped the wall to gain my balance. It was day 197 on my journey. It is a day I will never forget.

✎ MARKER MESSAGE

Now that you have experienced the bottom, gather your tools to climb higher. Each day requires you to put in the work to move from your current state. Find joy in the simple things, and most importantly, forgive yourself and others. Let joy light your path as you begin again. It is ok to start from the bottom, just remember to start and not stay there.

STARTED FROM THE BOTTOM

MARKERS OF JOY

I. There are signs along the way, that change is coming.

Change is the only constant that exists. Seasons change, people change, and your life will change as well. Change may be uncomfortable, but it is not always bad. There may be foreshadows that are informing you of the presence of change, but you must look and listen.

    A. What do you want, you get to choose.

    B. Listen to wise counsel, they may see further than you.

    C. Do not limit yourself, the best is yet to come.

II. You do not have to write the end of the story, just the next page.

At this point, make small decisions. Take the walk, one step at a time. Do not try to do this alone. Talk to others and let them know what you are thinking. Embrace the opportunity.

    A. Remember, you are equipped. Examine your tools and let them reveal your path.

MARKER MESSAGE

B. Use your network. Mentors, ambassadors, and sponsors are necessary on the journey.

C. Who are you? This is your chance to be you, do not blow it by pretending to be someone else.

III. Healing is a process – no step can be skipped.

If you have been hurt or traumatized by past occurrences, you must deal with it. Stop pretending that it is fine. It is not, and you cannot hide it. The eggs will crack and stink eventually.

A. Forgive the process and free those who played a role. Free yourself.

B. Mindset matters. Think joy, favor, and winning.

C. Enjoy the journey. Look for the beauty around as you LIVE LOVE.

CHAPTER 3
<u>DID THE BOTTOM</u>
<u>FALL OUT?</u>

The ride of your life, may be a rollercoaster. Buckle up, because the next drop will likely take your breath away!

When I hit rock bottom, I was certain that things were as bad as they could be. I faced my wilderness experience and worked to be better. I changed my thoughts, behaviors, and outlook on life. I felt wonderful and faithful about a greater future. But something was wrong!

"Hello doctor, how are you? Now is a good time. Yes, I can talk. Let me go back into the house so I can hear better. What did you just say?"

I could not believe my ears.

I went to my annual check-up expecting to brag about my tremendous weight loss and new found healthier me. My doctor was now on the phone telling me something else.

He began to explain, "We ran the tests again. I wanted to be sure. I am so sorry."

My heart began to race. My hands were shaking. I sat on the bed and braced myself. "You are sorry, doctor what is going on?"

He took a deep breath and said with a sorrowful tone, "You have leukemia. I know you feel healthy right now, but this is serious. We have to address this immediately."

I remember looking around my bedroom. Where was I? What was happening? I was hoping to see something that let me know that I was in the wrong place. This was not my home and therefore not my life. This was not my diagnosis. This was not happening to me.

The doctor continued speaking, but I was not hearing him now. How could this be?

I asked him, "What happened? How did this happen to me?"

He began to explain the specifics of my diagnosis and tell me the technical information related to my condition. He discussed the tests and how fortunate I was to have come in for my check-up, especially since I had no symptoms. I was devastated. I had a mix of emotions. I was fearful, angry, confused, and in disbelief.

As he spoke, I heard a voice from inside, "This is not unto death." At that moment a single tear ran down my cheek. The fear and anger that was rising, began to subside. It was replaced with hope and faith. I believed the voice despite the conversation unfolding. I took a deep breath and said, "Ok doc, what are we going to do, because I do not have time for cancer!" He explained to me that my disease was caused by a chromosomal abnormality and an oncologist would be needed.

That was great news to me. My confidence grew even stronger. I said to him, "Doctor I have faith. This is on a chromosomal level? Well God knew about that. I cannot worry myself about a glitch happening at that level of my being. And secondly, my sister is an oncologist. I am going to be fine."

By the end of the conversation, I wanted to console my doctor. He was distressed about my condition and concerned about my lack of distress. He probably thought I was in shock. I heard him just fine. I heard everything I needed to hear.

In addition to the voice inside, providing me peace, I found markers of joy in his delivery of the news. I looked for the messages to point me in the right direction. "Chromosomal Abnormality," told me that God allowed a glitch to reside to be revealed at this moment. The glitch was placed in the journey path at the point of my conception and revealed itself on schedule. This was predetermined. This was a necessary part of my destiny.

To need an oncologist, which was my sister's specialty, was ideal. I had a personal connection to an expert that was not only gifted in the field but loved me personally. As my doctor was speaking, a separate message was playing from my spirit. What I heard was, destined, purposed, permitted, and companionship. Those messages told me that I was not in control, but the one who was had it all in order. This moment in time was not by accident and it was my moment in time.

This will forever be marked as my D-Day (Diagnosis Day). At that moment I declared favor over my life. I spoke what I expected to happen. I chose life and that was non-negotiable. I had a diagnosis of my own! I hung up the phone and began planning to live. I may have had cancer, but cancer was not going to have me!

SHARING THE NEWS

I understood the urgency of the matter. I was not going to sit and do nothing. But I had decided that falling apart, was not on the to-do list today. I called my sister, the oncologist,

"Hey Sis. I need to talk to you." She said, "Can I call you back I am doing rounds?"

Normally I would have said yes and waited patiently for her to return my call, but today I needed her. I needed her immediately. I was not willing to wait in line or take a number.

"No, they are already in the hospital. I need you now," I responded.

My tone was serious, and she did not question my urgency. She replied, "Oh, ok, let me step away for a second. What is going on?"

I took a deep breath and explained the call from my doctor, "Sis, he said I have Leukemia."

She screamed through the phone, "WHAT? When? Start from the beginning."

I replayed the conversation with my doctor, at least the parts I could remember.

As I heard myself share the diagnosis, I began to cry. Tears ran down my cheeks and I found it hard to breath. I was telling my sister that I had cancer.

"Ok, calm down. Send me all the test results and information from the hospital. I will look at it and call you back. You are going to be fine. I have got you. This is what I do!"

She is my sister by marriage, and we are close. Although she is my younger sister, I felt like the kid sister at that moment. I needed her to handle this. I had no idea where to begin. I was out of my area of expertise for sure. The doctor was in the house, and I was grateful.

I responded, "Thank you sis. I need one favor, do not tell anyone. You are the only person that knows. I need some time to process what is going on." She promised to keep this between us, for now. I knew the request was difficult, you see, she was married to my younger brother. He and I loved each other very much. She knew he would be worried and would want to know. I just needed a little more time with this, before involving everyone else.

I sat and prayed. First, I was grateful for my life and my experiences up to this date. I was thankful for the phone call to remind me of my annual physical and the need to make an appointment. I was accepting of what was to come. I no longer feared uncertainty. I now also knew that what I thought was Rock Bottom, was not the lowest point possible. The diagnosis was a downward spiral I did not see coming.

I had always heard, "Be careful what you say. Your words have power." There is a scripture in the Bible that speaks of the power of the tongue (Proverbs 18:21 NIV). The power of life and death resides in your words. I was not prepared to declare death on myself, but the word cancer scared me to my core.

THE BIG C

I was first introduced to cancer while in college, more than 20 years ago. It was at this time, the word cancer, became a being; a living, breathing existence in my life. My grandmother was diagnosed. She was my friend, confidant, and cheerleader. She now had that thing they called cancer. I witnessed her struggle as her breathing became challenging which caused her to need oxygen. I vividly remember during one of my visits to Arizona, witnessing her drag that tank everywhere she went. Cancer gave her this companion that never left her side. I knew she was ill, but I did not realize how severe her health issues were. I remember speaking very nonchalantly about her condition. I had returned from a visit in Arizona and told a friend about it. I was so happy to see my grandma. I told him that she and her cancer are doing fine. I spoke of cancer like it was her buddy. I remarked about it as if she had invited cancer over to be a house guest. I now know that when you are told that you have cancer, you do not roll out the welcome mat and invite it in!

I had just finished a major project and wanted to tell my grandma that I did well. The phone rang, and my grandfather answered the phone. I was full of excitement, I did not notice his tone. I asked to speak to my grandmother. He said she could not come to the phone. That was not a problem to me. I replied, "Ok, tell her to call me back when she gets a minute. I have something to tell her." My grandfather replied in a tone that was almost harsh and full of frustration, "No she cannot come to the phone, she is gone." The way he spoke those words, sent chills down my spine. I was not thinking she was running an errand, or maybe that they had a spat. I knew this meant something else, but I could not wrap my mind around what he was saying. With tears and sorrow, my grandfather said, "I'm sorry, there was nothing left to do. She is no longer in pain. She is at rest now."

As my mind comprehended what I was being told, my knees buckled, my stomach ached, and I screamed at the top of my lungs! My grandmother was dead. My friend was gone, and cancer did it! I ached in ways that an aspirin could not relieve, a hug could not lessen, and words could not console. I had never hurt like this before. I had not experienced death of someone this close to me. And honestly, I did not realize that cancer could do this! Cancer killed my grandmother and I was not prepared. I HATE CANCER!

I would later lose both my grandfathers and my dad to that bastard cancer! Unfortunately, I had come to believe that cancer had an associated death sentence that could not be avoided. I was terrified of this diagnosis.

When my father was diagnosed, he was given six months to live. Because of my prior experience with my grandmother, I went into planning mode. My dad and I had a few unresolved conflicts and I did not want this to be carried into our final days. So, we developed a plan. My dad came to visit me with a single agenda, let us get things right with each other. When dad came to visit, it was as if I was a little girl, full of anticipation and joy. I was 34 years old, but I was still a daddy's girl. We laughed, cried, played, danced, and talked. We talked about past hurts. We talked about mistakes and misunderstandings. At that moment we had adult conversations that resisted the urge to look good and save face. Instead we told the ugly truth. We were honest with each other and open to apologize for wrongs. I felt complete. I felt understood. I felt loved. The little girl that felt abandoned and disappointed finally received the apology she longed for. My father died a few weeks later. It has only been a total of 90 days from when I was originally notified about his condition. Cancer does not follow the rules. I was promised 6 months. We were going on a cruise and were going to watch a sunrise together. Who hit fast forward and robbed me of my time? Oh, yes, cancer!

You see, cancer is not just the fear of death. For me, it is the uncertainty of time. It is the inclusion of pain. I was worried about everything from losing my hair to losing the very life I had finally vowed to live in love. Cancer was not welcome in my life. Being at rock bottom would have been an upgrade for me. This was far worse! The bottom had fallen out!

OBLIGATIONS

I cleaned my tear covered faced and went back to the garage to finish loading my car. That is what I was doing when my doctor called. Although I had been given a new set of circumstances to comprehend, I had life obligations made before I received the phone call from my doctor, just hours earlier. I agreed to showcase my business and LIVE LOVE brand. The event was the next day. My desire to help others

LIVE LOVE had now received a sense of urgency. I had a message to share and a hope that all those I encountered would understand the importance.

The next morning, I was different. I had received a new lens in which to view – everything. When I awoke, I paused and smiled. I realized that I was given another day. I had not died in my sleep. I took a deep breath and said, "Good morning world." The action of taking the breath meant something. I took that breath for my grandmother who was no longer around. I inhaled in her honor. As I prepared for the day, I took a glance in the mirror, I smiled and told my dad – I am going to make you proud! In honor of him, I was going to face the crowd and spread love to them all. I found strength in their absence. I felt obligated to make them proud. I felt like they were with me, cheering me on. I had cancer, but cancer did not have me. I praised my God for that. I was alive and ready to live.

It was ironic that I spent my day convincing others to join my LIVE LOVE movement, while internalizing the fact that I was entering a fight for my life.

Leukemia is a cancer that affects the blood. There are several types of leukemia. Some are more severe than others. All require treatment and each person's experience is unique to their body and personal health. My annual exam saved my life. I had no symptoms. Do not leave your health to chance, know your status.

I believed the voice that spoke to me the day before, "This is not unto death." I decided that instead of getting busy dying, I was going to get busy living!

CHANGE OF PLANS

After a successful debut, I began to blog about my daily actions of LIVE LOVE and encouraged others to post as well. I reengaged in my mindfulness walks. The Wisconsin terrain was not as gorgeous as my Arizona experience, but the walks were exhilarating. I communed with nature, received input and messages from street signs, and was inspired by every walk I completed. This also helped me maintain the weight loss I experienced in Arizona.

It had been three weeks since my diagnosis and I began preparation for my move to Arizona. The relocation plan included the selling of my home in Wisconsin. I completed my home appraisal and had 3 people interested in the property. The excitement of relocating took my mind off the health situation. I had not begun treatment, and I had no symptoms, so it was like the call never happened. That is what I told myself, at least for the moment. Once I completed the sale of my home, I would retreat to my desert oasis and begin my new life. I knew that treatment would begin, and I would need to address the leukemia, but being in Arizona would add the perfect scenery to this next journey.

Over the course of a few weeks, I experienced set backs on the home sale. The numbers were not making sense. The prospective buyers were each having difficulties in securing their finances. It was as if the entire plan was unraveling. I had a sure thing and now nothing seemed to line up.

I was frustrated and confused. I prayed about this move. I wanted this move. Why was this not working out for me? Did I miss something? I walked into my garage which had become the resting place for all the boxes that were packed and moving to the desert. I stood in the garage and viewed the boxes that were packed and piled against the wall. My friends and I had successfully packed everything I owned that I did not need for daily existence. All my decorations, candles, pictures, and excess clothing sat neatly in my garage waiting to be loaded and taken away. There were more than 40 boxes in the garage. Now it seemed as if the sale of my home was not going to occur. I could not afford to move without completing the sale. I felt defeated, disappointed, and confused. I decided to have a chat with God.

"Lord, I know that your way is easy. I never have to struggle when I am in alignment with your will. Why is this so hard? And if you did not want me to move, why in the world did you have me pack all this crap?"

I was now angry and wanted an answer to my question.

I received an answer. I heard God say, "There are doors for you to walk through, but you need to be here to do so."

Ok, that answered the question about me not moving, but I still wanted a response about the boxes. Why are my belongings sitting in the garage? I wanted to know the purpose of this wasteful exercise. We had spent weeks carefully wrapping, packing, and even purging items. I donated truckloads of my personal belongings. I felt bamboozled! I sat and stared at the boxes. It was as if I expected them to know the response to my question. After sitting thirty minutes, evaluating my frustration, and repenting for my anger, I asked again.

"God, I thank you for the doors that you have prepared for me. I just do not understand why I packed up my life to stay put!"

I received my answer. I heard God say, "Your life needs to declutter. It is time to make room for the new."

Now at this point in my life, I am comfortable having

conversations with God. And yes, I hear him. I may not listen, but I do hear him each time. I heard him, but I did not understand.

"Make room for new?"

I figured more would be revealed later. It was nice outside; my car would be fine. I hoped a clearer answer would come before the first snow! My desert oasis would have to wait, and my life is being decluttered? I had not planned for this. If I was not moving to Arizona, where was I going? I was making room for new, but what I had was serving me perfectly fine. I was confused, but willing to comply. This is still the year of favor!

CLOSER LOOK

Five weeks after my initial leukemia diagnosis was my scheduled biopsy. This procedure would allow the medical team to take a closer look at the impact Leukemia was having on my system. This bone marrow biopsy was the next step in the plan. It was time for me to begin treatment and this had to be completed first. My mom agreed to join me for the procedure. Although it was simply an exploratory step in my process, I was a bit nervous. My life was about to change, and I had no control over the next steps.

The week of the procedure was a busy time for me. I planned to serve as a vendor at my church's conference. My LIVE LOVE debut had been successful, and I planned to build on the momentum. I had it all mapped out. I would go in for the procedure and rest that evening. I also began chemotherapy the day after the procedure. That would require me to allow for additional rest the next day, but I could attend the church conference in the evening. My mom felt my plan was aggressive, but I believed I could handle it. We just needed to follow the plan and it would all be fine. Wednesday,

Thursday, Friday – all was set.

I consider my planning skills as one of my strengths. It is also one of the biggest obstacles for me as well. If you have had any type of life experiences, you know that you can never plan for everything that life will throw your way. For some reason, I continue to forget!

The biopsy preparation was an interesting experience. The number of people in the room made me feel that I was about to experience something rather serious. Everyone introduced themselves and their role. I looked at my mom and said, "Did you get that? Are you taking attendance?" We all laughed, and I had my first procedure as a cancer patient.

That evening was difficult. I had problems getting comfortable. I was in pain and my mind was racing thinking about tomorrow. Chemotherapy. The name is intimidating. Although everyone attempted to ease my stress, I was worried.

The soundbites that you experience while dealing with difficult situations can be interesting. I was told by at least three different medical professionals, "If you had to have cancer, this is the one you want." I understand what they were saying, and everyone was attempting to be helpful, but let us examine this dialogue.

"If you have to have cancer, this is the one you want."

First, why would I have to have cancer? That is ridiculous. I must have air, water, and food. I will never have to have cancer. Second, this will never be the one I want. You can keep all this. I did not get in line, walk up to the counter, and speculate over the menu of cancer options. I do not want this. If you feel this way, you take it!

Of course, I would not wish this situation on anyone. I just needed to share the thoughts that ran through my mind as I laid in pain, post biopsy, after the anesthesia and good meds wore off.

The morning would bring another chapter to my journey, chemo. After long discussions with my medical team, I was comfortable with our choice and hoped for limited side effects. I was eager to begin, simply to eliminate and dismiss my old friend – uncertainty.

FIRST TIME

The birds chirped loudly. The sun shined brightly. It was the day to begin chemo. To be honest, other than the discomfort from the biopsy, I had not experienced any of the pain described by the doctors. I was grateful and ready. I was ready to begin the treatment that would eradicate the Big C. I had created a personification for cancer. Cancer was represented by an oversized, sloppily dressed, bully. One that always picked on those smaller. One who was not as tough as initially thought and could be defeated. I created this visual, so my enemy would feel more real.

Although it was a beautiful day, I felt horrible. I did not sleep well and my entire skeleton ached. My doctor had described a symptom called bone pain. I had not experienced this problem – until now. My body hurt from the inside. This was not like a muscle spasm, or even a cut on the skin; this pain radiated from a place I had never felt before. The pain was deep and intense. The surge of discomfort took my breath away. I took my medication with the hope that it would somehow reduce my pain. The attack needed to begin immediately. The enemy was gaining ground and I needed my troops to go in and stop the advance. I therefore embraced my inaugural dose of chemo-therapy.

I sat and waited for something to happen. I am not sure what I expected, but I expected something. After sitting for twenty minutes, I decided to return to sleep. I was tired and could use a little more rest. I figured a few hours of sleep would be all I needed. I was still planning to attend the church conference later that evening. I had a vendor booth waiting for me. Stick to the plan.

Although I was moving slowly, my mom accompanied me to the church. I also invited a good friend, in case I needed extra help. The parking lot was busy which made unloading a bit difficult. We pulled to the front door and decided to give it a try. Of course, I was no help. I could barely walk and could not lift anything, but I was committed to the plan – my plan.

As we unloaded the car, my mom looked for someone to help. I heard a familiar voice approaching but was confused as to the owner. Standing at the trunk of the car, helping unload was my friend, Clark. I had not spoken to him since he moved, over a month ago. I thought he was in Texas. As he approached me, carrying the items my mother had given him, he looked at me and smiled. "We need to talk," was all he said as he passed.

I was happy to see him but confused by his presence. I know he had not come back to town for the conference. I also wondered what we needed to talk about. All of that would have to wait, because as I watched him unload the car, I realized my attendance was a big mistake. My body ached, and I did not feel well. My plan was not working as I expected. It is time for plan B. I need to go home and try this again tomorrow.

I did not accept defeat and did not tell my mother of my agony. I attempted to endure and stay for the service. After an hour, I realized it was time for a new plan, indeed.

My mother looked at me, and without asking said, "I knew this was going to be too much. We need to get you back to bed." I did not put up a fight. As we were having the discussion, Clark walked by the table. My mom updated him on the plan and asked him to assist. He agreed and loaded the items back into the car. He asked me if I was ok. I replied, "I will be. I just need to rest." He was at the right place at the right time. I appreciated him for that.

THE MIGRAINE

After the ordeal the night before, I decided to stay in bed the entire day and rest. With a full day of rest, I could attend the night service without feeling drained. That morning, I ate breakfast, took my medications and headed back to bed.

My slumber only lasted an hour. My sleep was interrupted by pain more intense than the pains of the previous day. I was being tortured from the inside out.

I could not lay on my back because the swelling from the biopsy felt like a knife cutting into my tailbone. I tried to lay on my side, but my legs and arms throbbed with pain and felt hot, almost on fire. I tried to lay on my stomach, but a new pain emerged. I experienced a migraine amid everything else. Nausea, ear throbbing, light sensitivity, and the feeling that someone had taken a sledge hammer to my temple was now an added torture episode. I screamed, cried, and balled up on my knees. The pain was so severe I doubled up my pain medication and passed out. I must have slept for eight or nine hours. My mom came into the room as she heard me moving around. "How do you feel," she asked. I felt better but my head was sore. That was the worst migraine I ever experienced!

"I am ok now. That was too intense! What time is it? I want to go back to church," I replied. She looked at me with worry on her face, "Are you sure you should be doing this?" I was not sure, but I needed to go back to church. I needed to not stay home sick. I refused to give in. Keeping my emotions in check was very important to me. I accepted that I was dealing with a medical situation. I acknowledged that I had new components to my life. I, however, refused to be sick. Anything that felt like sickness, was not going to work for me. Staying in bed, was on the list of things sick people do. No thank you. I just had to convince my mother that I was not sick.

"I will not go back to be a vendor, I just want to go for service. It is Friday night and I do not want to miss it. Let us go and just have a seat. I promise, if I feel anything, we are headed to the door and I will come back home without a fight." She seemed agreeable to my amended plan. So, we dressed and headed to church.

News of my diagnosis had not been shared with my church members. I was not prepared for them to know. I had just become comfortable with my immediate family knowing. I was still wrapping my head around the matter. I was fighting this battle in silence. I had not requested the prayers of the church. I was not looking for someone to visit me at home and check on me. I just needed to cross this hurdle and I would be fine.

We arrived at the church and were immediately greeted with hugs and warm wishes. One member asked, "I thought I saw you yesterday, but then you were gone." I smiled and replied, "Yes, I headed home early. But I am back today and am so glad to see you." That is all she needed to know. Nothing more to be said.

My mother and I sat in the back of the sanctuary so that I would not have to walk too far. It was also convenient if we needed to leave. I looked at my mom and smiled, "Thank you for being here. I could not do this without you." She leaned over and hugged me. I needed that hug.

The service began, and the sanctuary erupted. There were hundreds of people excited to celebrate God. The energy was flowing through the crowd. I sat in the sea of love and added my gratitude to the atmosphere. I am here. I am alive. I am glad.

As the music played, a pain developed in my ears. I did not think about my sound sensitivity. I put tissue in my ears to block the vibrations. It helped a little. As the choir sang, the lights seemed brighter than normal. I added sun shades to my ensemble. Of course, light and noise are never a good mix with a migraine. As I sat and listened to the announcements, I could not understand what was being said. It was like another language was being spoken. Something was happening to me. Before panicking, I decided that a trip to the restroom was needed. A little water on my face, would calm down my senses. I told my mom where I was headed and began my slow stroll to the restroom. As I walked down the hall, I believed that the restroom was moving further away with every step. At this point, I was sweating, and my hands were shaking. I abandoned the restroom plan. I decided to go get some air. That door was close enough to me to reach it safely. I walked outside to the parking lot. I saw people walking around, but I could not say anything to them. I felt unstable both physically and mentally. Coming outside proved to be an unwise choice. I felt myself becoming confused and overwhelmed.

I was experiencing a mental breakdown. I was in pain, discombobulated and afraid. This felt like the seizures I had as a teen. I was not prepared for this. What was happening to me? The crowds continued to pour into the church. I needed to stand away from the crowd.

I stood on the edge of the curb and looked out to the parking lot. If I focus on something in the distance, maybe I can calm down and ask for help. My mother was inside and did not know what was happening.

"What is going on," I heard a voice ask. This voice was familiar. As I focused, I realized it was Clark walking across the parking lot. Where had he come from? I looked at him and said, "I do not know." I began to cry, and he stood there and held me. I could hear him giving instructions and talking to those around us. All I could do was cry. My head was throbbing, my body ached, I was confused and afraid. I was sick, and I could not deny it.

As I stood in agony, I realized that my friend continued to show up every time I needed him. It was at this moment, I named him Clark. I felt like I had my own personal Superman. He kept arriving just in time. Clark Kent held me in his arms and made everything calm.

As my mom came out of the church, someone was pulling up in my car. Clark walked me to the car and helped me get in. He reached over me to fasten my seat belt, looked at my mom and said, "Call me if you need anything. She has the number." Oddly enough, my panic was subsiding, and I felt like myself again, just in time to hear his remark. I smiled and rolled my eyes. Was he using this moment to flirt? Was he doing so in front of my mother? He was right, I had the number. I smiled as we drove away. My mom asked, "So who is he?" I looked at her and said, "Please drive."

We made it home safely, but the pain did not end. The debilitating headache lasted seven days. Imagine waking up to the feeling that your ears, eyes, and brain were about to explode. The only way to make it through the day was by medicating to the point of unconsciousness. This was my routine for a week. I did not want to eat. I did not talk on the phone or look at television. I took medicine and slept. I woke up on the eighth day and the headache was gone. I am not sure what made it stop, I was just glad it did.

My mother joined me at my first follow-up appointment. The headache was gone, and my body seemed to be accepting the chemotherapy. This was my first time returning to the hospital since the biopsy. My new journey had begun. After checking in at the reception desk, she asked us if we knew where to go. I replied, "No ma'am this is my first visit." She smiled and said, "I understand, let me have a guide take you to the right elevator." I thought that was incredible customer service. My mom and I walked with the guide who pointed to a hall and said, "This is where you want to go." We thanked the guide and walked towards the elevator. As we walked down the hall, I was slapped by reality. The sign was colorful and creative, but the words did not bring me joy – CANCER CENTER.

It was the first time I saw the words written out. There was no turning back. It was official. As I entered the elevator that was down the special hallway, so tucked away you needed a guide – I comprehended that I had cancer. My mother and I rode the elevator in silence. A tear rolled down my cheek. She grabbed my hand and held it. She too realized that her oldest child was a cancer patient and there was nothing she could do about it.

I looked back on my love affair with my job and realized that I had more important things to love. At the top of the list was my life! This marked journey day 238. I had a new priority list and at the top of it was me.

✎ MARKER MESSAGE

Life can be unpredictable. Just as you see the light at the end of the tunnel, life can throw you a curve ball. The rules seem to have changed. How can something else be added to the story? The original situation was bad enough, but now this? Please remember that you will not be faced with more than you can handle. It will not feel like it at the time, but you can handle this too. There are those who will come to your aid. Let them in. Let them assist you. It is not selfish. It is love. Let love in.

DID THE BOTTOM FALL OUT?

MARKERS OF JOY

I. When given an accelerated timetable, treat it as the gift that it is. Now you know, you do not have time to waste. Keep things in perspective. Do not sweat the small stuff.

    A. I have been told that I am patient and have a calming way about me. To be honest, I have a marker to measure everything against. When faced with an issue, I ask myself, "Is this worse than Leukemia?" It is amazing how my perspective has changed. You see, Leukemia is bad, and I have no choice but to go through and persevere. The worst news has not been as bad as that. So, there is no reason for me to lose my cool about the minor issues in my life. I need to keep a clear head for the majors! Identify your life's measuring rod.

    B. What is your marker to measure major or minor

MARKER MESSAGE

against? How does the issue stack up? You have been through worse. You may be going through worse right now. Find joy in remembering that you can handle the major.

II. There is a saying, "No man is an island."

There is someone who cares. That someone may be related to you or a neighbor. The support may come from a significant other or a friend. Your help may be provided by a social service organization or your church. The point is, do not attempt to navigate life issues alone. Let someone in. Others are blessed through service. Allow them to serve you.

A. To be served by others, pride must be eliminated. It is not honorable believing that you do not need anyone. It is an act of selfishness. People feel better when they help others. Your problems are put in perspective when someone shares theirs. Your strength may be the testimony that someone else needs to witness to know that they can make it.

B. I believe life experiences serve two purposes. The first is so that we can learn, grow, and believe. After surviving an extreme experience your muscle of faith is exercised. You now know what it is like to go through a storm. You also know what it is like to survive. The second purpose is to help others. Your experience is not unique to you. Someone needs to know your experience because they are having a similar experience and do not know how they are going to make it. Hearing how you made it, will help

MARKER MESSAGE

them. Share your story.

III. Take a loved one to the doctor and be sure to keep your appointment as well.

We ignore warning signs and assume it will go away. Even worse, there are some issues that are not detectable or show no symptoms. Do not leave your health to chance. You have too much life to live to be a walking time bomb. It takes more than an apple a day to keep the doctor away. Are all your check-ups up to date? Go and Know.

CHAPTER 4
THINGS ARE LOOKING UP!

At your lowest point, you must look up. Focus on where you want to be, not on where you are.

The life I knew before June 23rd – "D Day," is no more. That phone call changed my life. I accepted that reality, but I also decided that I would determine how it changed my life. I decided that it would change my life for the better. I was not certain what was going to be better, but I surely refused to accept anything worse!

RESET

I had established a routine while living in Arizona. My life would now need a reset to ensure I was properly dealing with my current health situation. Daily chemotherapy was my new normal. I did not have any noticeable side effects and my energy had increased significantly. I wanted to stay on my path to a healthier me, so I hired a physical trainer. If I had to work through Leukemia, I would minimize any other unhealthy components of my life. During my doctor's appointment we discussed the importance of a healthy lifestyle.

I thought about how unhealthy I had become prior to going to Arizona. Reality hit me. Leaving my beloved job, saved my life. My mind and body were in no condition to deal with my present situation. If the blood cancer did not kill me, the stress would have caused such a mental breakdown. Who knows what I would have done. It does not matter. None of that happened. Looking back, I was saved by abandoning ship. I now can live to sail another day. I was grateful!

While in Arizona, I adopted a casual attire. I put away the business suits and began to dress down a bit. It had been nearly ten years since I owned a true business casual wardrobe. I typically did not dress down on the weekends either. People noticed the change. I received multiple compliments. "Love the new look. I did not even recognize you! Wow, whatever you are doing, keep it up!" People embraced the wardrobe reset as well.

I found the compliments both flattering and interesting. I did not look like what I was going through. That was a rewarding feeling. I did not want to look sick. I did not want to appear ill. I wanted to be seen living and loving every moment of it. It was important for me to continue to LIVE LOVE out loud. I was walking in purpose and it brought me joy in the midst of my pain. That's right, I had cancer. I almost forgot.

I began to invite others to walk with me. We would select different paths and explore various neighborhoods. We would laugh, talk, sing, and enjoy each other's company. I looked forward to my daily walks. I was excited about the strength I was developing. It showed during my training appointments. I was able to pick up heavier weights and endure longer workouts. My body also showed the difference. I had curves! Now, to be honest, I had curves before, but they were much like the curves on your friendly neighborhood snowman – all curving outward. Now I had better proportions and had girly curves. Not only did I feel healthier, I felt sexy. That feeling had been absent for more than 15 years. Yes, I was bringing sexy back!

I believed that something great was heading my way. I was not sure what, but I told everyone I knew, "I am about to walk into a blessing like none other!" I had faith and worked daily to keep my thoughts positive.

The Bible says, "If you believe, you will receive whatever you ask for in prayer." (Matthew 21:22 NIV) Of course, there are some pre-requisites to this scripture. I cannot pray for something that does not align with God's will. I was not worried about that. I wanted to see the miraculous. I believed that my positive thoughts would attract positivity to me. My joy seemed to cause others to be happy. My smile made others smile. Why not spread positivity as well? I think, therefore I am.

WATCH THIS

I was asked how I kept such a positive attitude during such a scary time in my life. I had history. This was not the first time I faced a negative situation. This was also not the first time I faced a negative medical diagnosis. Each time, I grew spiritually and grew in faith. I knew the only way I made it through those previous circumstances was with God. He did not leave me in turmoil then, so I did not expect to be left now. My attitude was, "Let us see what God is going to do with this one!"

Allow me to share a bit of my medical journey.

At the age of 17, I was infected with Shingles. There was no vaccine and there was not as much knowledge about the disease back then. The doctor kept telling me it was a disease that normally affected older adults. I remember laughing telling him, "When I was 3, I stayed with my great-grandmother in the senior citizen complex. The neighbors called me the world's youngest senior citizen. I was always a young old person!"

The shingles outbreak occurred normally at first. After a couple of weeks, instead of clearing up as expected the rash continued to spread until it covered half of my torso. My entire right side was blistered. In addition to the painful sores, I began to experience numbness in my right foot. The feeling was like the tingle you get when your foot falls asleep. It felt like needles were sticking my foot. After a few days, the tingle was in my right leg as well. After a week, my entire right side felt numb to the touch, but had the painful needle prick feeling.

I had successfully infected my 3 younger siblings with chicken-pox and I was developing mobility issues. My poor mother had a house full of itchy kids. After a week, my younger siblings returned to school. I, however, was now experiencing numbness on my left side. My foot and lower leg were being attacked. I needed help moving around and only had use of my left hand at this point. My mom decided that I would have to stay with my grandmother during the day. She did not want me left alone. She informed me that she would begin dropping me off the next day. This was prior to my grandparents' move to Arizona. I frequented their house weekly. I went to bed to rest for tomorrow's adventure. I had been out of school for almost a month at that point. I looked forward to company during the day. I was lonely.

My mom woke me up the next morning. She was very hurried and was giving orders from the other room. "Go ahead and get up. I need to drop you off. Breakfast is in the kitchen. You really need to try and eat something. Get a move on, we have to go." I tried to get out of bed, but I could not get up. I tried, but all I felt was the sticking of needles all over my body. My mom came into the room. She was about to start fussing, but she looked at me and asked, "Are you feeling ok?" I am not sure what she saw but I felt horrible. She grabbed my hand

and felt it. When she let it go, my hand fell towards the floor and hit the side of the bed. She looked at me in horror. I could not move my arm. My left arm was now immobile like my right. I had no motor skills beyond my head.

My mom grabbed a pin and stuck my arm. She asked, "do you feel that?" I shook my head no. She poked my leg. I shook my head no. As she prepared to stick me again I said, "Listen, I cannot feel anything, but I do not want to be a pin cushion either! Stop sticking me."

I did not see my grandmother that day. Instead, I was rushed to the hospital. Something was going on beyond the itchy shingles. The admitting doctor asked a few questions before admitting me, "What have you eaten?" I replied, "An orange and a beef sandwich." My mom interjected, "That was a week ago. You have not eaten in a week?" I had lost my appetite and feeding myself had become difficult. I did what many normal teenagers would do. I lied! I reported eating daily, but it was not true. I did not want to appear helpless, so I just did not tell her.

The doctor then asked if I had vomited or passed out? I told him, "No, but can I have some water?" The nurse brought me a cup of water, which my mother had to hold for me. She held the cup and straw, but also continued lecturing me about lying to her. I interrupted her and said, "Ok, I am sorry, but I do not feel good. Can we talk about this later?" At that moment the water was regurgitated, and I passed out. I woke up in ICU two days later. It turns out my shingles infection was classified as internal shingles, which meant the virus was attacking other systems in my body. My organs were shutting down.

When I awoke, the doctor updated me on my condition. He also informed me that I was experiencing paralysis and tests were needed.

At the age of seventeen, I was a high school senior. I was co-captain of my school's pompon squad. I was accepted to my chosen college and received a full scholarship. What did he mean, I was paralyzed? I did not return to school. For six months I fought an emotional and physical battle. There seemed to be so many elements working against me. I was not sure I would survive.

I was eventually moved from the hospital to a rehabilitation facility once the doctors believed my condition had improved. I did not like the facility. It was far away from my home which meant my mother could not visit me. There were no other children in the facility; and the place had a weird smell! I participated in daily activities to improve my condition. I had physical therapy, psychotherapy, and occupational therapy multiple times a week.

I was afraid, angry, defiant – Seventeen! I had days of outbursts. They kept talking to me as if I would never walk again. They talked to me as if I was sick. I wanted to go home. I missed my family. I had not seen my friends in months. I was alone. To make matters worse, at night, when in bed, there were bed rails and cuffs to strap me to the bed. They said that my outbursts caused them concern and they did not want me to harm myself. Harm myself? I was paralyzed from the neck down. What was I going to do, blink myself to death? I hated the facility and it showed. The only bright spot was a kind family that would visit me when their family member was in therapy.

My time was cut short because they realized that I had begun to have Petit mal seizures, also known as Absence seizures. The shingles was not lying dormant, it was activated again and now my brain was under attack.

My mom came to the facility to escort me on the ambulance ride. As we left, I wanted to say goodbye to the family that kept me company. They were the only thing I would miss about my visit to rehab hell. Meeting that family was exactly what I needed.

One day, while lying in bed, I heard a girl's voice. I looked in the hall and a little girl was standing in my doorway smiling at me. She waved, and I said hello. She slowly walked into my room and began to look around. My mother decorated the room to look homey. There was a poster of me on the wall, from my pompon photos. There was a radio and a box of tapes that contained all my favorite songs. There were also games and puzzles too. If someone came to visit, they could entertain themselves. The girl that cleaned my room liked the same music as I did. I enjoyed when she came to visit. She would close the door and turn the music up. It was an enjoyable part of my day. It was the only enjoyable part of my day.

The little girl's mom came in and said, "I am so sorry she is bothering you." I was happy to have a visitor. I missed my little brothers and sister, so seeing her was a joy. I told the mom, "It is no bother. My family lives too far to visit, and I miss my siblings. I enjoy watching her play."

The mom and daughter visited me several other times. When the dad was in therapy and they were waiting for him to return, they would sit and talk to me. They became my new moment of joy. I could not see my family, but I saw my new friends and that made me happy.

As we were leaving, I wanted my mom to say good-bye and thank the family for visiting me. Because of them, I was not lonely. I found my joy while in that horrible place.

The nurse pulled my mom to the side. I thought she was taking down the message for the family, but the way my mom looked over at me told me they were discussing something else. My mom walked back over, and I asked, "What did she say? Is she not going to tell them what I said?"

My mom looked at me with tears in her eyes and said, "Baby that is why I am here to get you. Your seizures are getting worse. There has been no family visiting you. You have not had any visitors since we last came." My mom and the nurse were confused. I know that my friends visited me. They came and listened to music. They sat and played games. We even talked.

Years later I revisited this scenario and realized that God took care of me in my time of need. I was a teenager in a strange place. I was afraid, depressed, and alone. During that time in my life, I learned the meaning of the bible verse Deuteronomy 31:6 (NIV), "Be strong and courageous. Do not be afraid or terrified because of them, for the Lord your God goes with you; he will never leave you nor forsake you."

I may have been having seizures and hallucinating, but I also know that I was visited by angels who kept me from being alone.

The doctors were wrong. It was a six-month journey, but I did walk again. I walked across my graduation stage. I walked onto the college campus. I walked into my future with an experience that forever changed me. I was stronger because of it.

Fifteen years later, my strength would be tested again.

Keep looking, just as you watched me walk again. Watch this…

EYE CHARTS

My experience with health challenges did not end there. My

father died in 2005 and I was under a significant amount of stress. While at work, I had a severe migraine. I completed my work day but had evening obligations as well. I was the Director of Vacation Bible School, for my church. This was the final evening of sessions. The only task left was the church picnic on Saturday. I believed I could endure one night of agony. The migraine would have to wait. While standing in front of the congregation, I noticed that my vision was blurry. I asked someone to read the evening passage since my vision was not cooperating. We continued with the program. The evening was successful. My team was ready to celebrate. Everyone went home and agreed to meet at the picnic location to set up in the morning.

I did not go directly home after church. There were a few items for me to grab at the store. As I drove to the store, my eyesight continued to be problematic. I did not wear glasses and had no previous eye issues. I was not sure what to make of this new situation. I completed my errands and went home to rest.

I woke the next morning very excited. This was my first time directing such a large project. I was proud of my team. The church members complimented us for an engaging week of activities. As I drove to the picnic site, my vision continued to be of issue. As I passed the mall, I decided to run into the eyewear shop in the mall. They were open on Saturday and accepted walk-ins.

The doctor saw me immediately. I explained what was happening and she agreed to check my vision. She had me look through a device and read the eye chart. It was blurry, but I could read the chart. She then covered one eye and instructed me to read the eye chart. I read the chart with no problem. She then covered my other eye and instructed me to read the eye chart. The dialogue that pursued confused us both.

"Ok ma'am read the eye chart," the doctor instructed.

"Ok," I responded as I waited for her to put the chart up for me to read.

"Alright ma'am read the chart," the doctor repeated.

"O. K.," I responded. I was waiting on her. Put the chart up already!

"Ma'am what do you see?" she asked.

"Nothing, when are you going to put the chart up?" I responded impatiently. Was this woman this incompetent? How was I going to read the chart if she did not put it up for me to see?

"Ma'am the chart is up," she responded with hesitation in her voice.

"NO, there is nothing up! The screen is black," I insisted.

The doctor turned the light on and looked into my eye. She then shined a light into my eye.

"Ma'am how did you get here? Is there someone who can drive you?" she asked.

"I drove, but my little sister is with me. She can drive. Where is she driving me?" I asked. At this point, I was thoroughly confused. She explained everything and ensured it was crystal clear.

"Ma'am you have lost your vision in your eye. You may have suffered a stroke or some sort of neurological damage. You must go to the emergency room immediately. We can call an ambulance, or your sister can drive you, but you need to go right now!"

Yes, I had lost my sight in my right eye. The blur was caused by my left eye attempting to see for the both. The day before, I had not closed one eye to see if it made a difference.

I had lost my vision and was unaware.

After going to the emergency room and being seen by multiple specialists, the doctor diagnosed me with Optic Neuritis. The swelling of the optic nerve caused me to lose sight in my eye. I had the pleasure of adding an eye patch to my daily ensemble. It took three months for me to regain my vision. I had a 90-day roller coaster ride. The treatment for my condition was a steroid treatment administered through a steroid IV infusion. The treatment lasted an hour and required an outpatient visit three times a week for three weeks. The steroid treatment caused me horrible pain in my joints. My muscles were weakened, and my joints ached. Eventually, in addition to the patch, a walker was added to my recovery tools. I could no longer stand on my own or walk across the room without the use of the walker. I could not see or walk.

Because of my previous paralysis, I had a comparison to determine how extreme this episode was to be considered. As I examined the facts, I concluded the following: It was only one eye. I could feel, even if I could not move on my own. This was only a six on my ten-point scale.

The day after treatment was always difficult. I felt fatigued and was in pain. That day was usually spent in the bed. Something very interesting began to happen. As I laid in bed and reminded myself of this only being a level six condition, I began to see things. This was not like the hallucinations from my teen years. No, I would see people that I knew. I could hear their concerns and issues. What was I supposed to do with this information?

While lying in bed I asked God, "Why do I see these things? What am I to do with this information?"

God instructed me to pray for them and with them.

I had no problem praying for them. I was involved in my

church and was very comfortable praying for others in need. However, praying with them would mean I had to call them. I had to tell them what I saw and heard? I was not too sure about that plan.

I prayed for the people. I saw a co-worker, a friend, and my mom. I laid in my bed and spoke to God on their behalf. After praying, I fell asleep as I normally did after treatment. As I slept, I kept seeing the same three people in my dream. This time, I not only heard their thoughts, I could feel their pain. I awoke confused and feeling guilty. I was not willing to risk embarrassment and having others think I was crazy. The pain I felt in my sleep was the agony of another. I had never felt this before and I was afraid to fall asleep and have this happen again.

I connected with all three. The co-worker was grateful. She said that she received confirmation that God heard her prayers. The friend shared that she did not want to burden me because of what I was going through. We laughed, talked, and cried together. I provided counsel, prayed with her and apologized for my delay. I was grateful to be allowed to be there for her. The biggest surprise was my mother.

I had lost contact with my mother for a period. After I graduated high school and left for college, my mother changed. She was struggling with life issues and drug abuse. She had withdrawn from the family. Her behavior was self-destructive and unhealthy. We had grown apart and I was not sure where she was living at the time. My brothers had left the house and I had custody of my little sister at this point. None of that mattered as I was faced with this current health crisis. She may not be in the best place, but at that time, I needed my mom.

I needed to let her know that she was loved and needed. I saw her in my dream. I called my brother to tell him what was going on. I told him that I needed mom. I needed her to know that I love her and needed her help. Not only did she receive the message, she jumped on a Greyhound bus and came to me. My mother nursed me back to health, attended my treatment appointments, and helped me move around. Although we had been estranged for a year, I had my mother back and it felt wonderful.

My eyesight recovered. My mother was back in my life, and she quit using drugs during that encounter. My obedience saved us both.

In the Bible the scripture Proverbs 3:5 (NIV) states, "Trust in the Lord with all your heart and lean not on your own understanding."

We do not know what caused the Optic Neuritis, but I know what happened because of it. After this experience, my ability to see the pain and concern of others remained. Yes, I feel the things they never speak. I experience their hurt as if it was happening to me. My current desire to help others LIVE LOVE is a selfish engagement. I want to rid the world of all hurt and pain so that no one ever hurts again. During this experience, I thanked God he chose to blind me, so I could see. That was another amazing "watch this" moment in my life!

I had numerous other encounters that were extreme. In the end, everything always works out for the best. In addition to working out for me, I have a new-found strength, faith, and closeness to God. From a muscle spasm to an ear ache. I hand it all over to God. So, when asked how I can keep my joy with such a terrifying diagnosis, I simply say – God. For me, it is an opportunity to see what he is going to do next.

It is foolish to think that you will not encounter fear.
Life is scary. Whether it is an uninvited spider or the
misplacement of something of value. Fear occurs in
our daily existence. The point is, put fear in its place.
Do not let it paralyze you and stop you from living.
Turn the situation over and watch God work. You may
be used in the solution but be found useful, not
fearful.

VERSIONS OF TRUTH

As you can see, because of my past experiences, I had a history
of overcoming adversity. I had experienced depths of hellish
situations and lived to see the other side of it all. My truth had
a version that may have seemed irrational and optimistic, but
for me it was an expected consistency. I am an overcomer
therefore I will overcome and that is my truth.

Life began to settle down and I had my new life on
schedule. I worked out with a personal trainer. I walked daily.
I was committed to LIVE LOVE out loud, and I had joy. My
outlook on life was positive and I felt peaceful.

My friend Clark had settled in after his return to
Wisconsin and reminded me that we needed to talk. It turns
out, that when I saw him at the church conference, he had just
returned from Texas, for good.

I was feeling much better and wanted to thank him for being
there for my mom and me. I called him up and asked him to
lunch. "Let me take you to lunch to thank you for being my
personal Superman." He accepted the lunch invitation and said
we would connect later in the week to figure out the details.

I was especially excited because my birthday was near. I
woke on a beautiful August morning and thanked God for the

chance to celebrate another year. This birthday would be special. I had no plans for next week, but I would celebrate somehow. Clark and I spoke and decided that we would have lunch on Thursday, August 3rd, which was five days before my birthday.

I rose Thursday morning excited about our outing. I would get to spend time with my friend. I would learn of his experience in Texas, as well as understand why he returned. I would also tell him the truth about my health.

As I prepared for the lunch I kept changing clothes. I could not figure out my wardrobe. I did not want to be too casual. I also did not want to look too sexy. I was confused, but more importantly, I realized that I cared. Why did my look matter so much on that day? I was trying to make a proper impression, but I was unsure of exactly what impression. As I looked around my room at the growing pile of clothes that marked my indecisiveness, I realized that I was interested in my friend. That made me nervous! I was not prepared for these feelings. I took a moment and talked myself off the ledge.

"Listen, it is just lunch. He has a girlfriend. He is your friend and you do not want to mess that up! Get a hold of yourself. Do not embarrass me!"

I calmed my nerves and drove to the agreed upon destination. We selected a restaurant that was outside of town. We both agreed that we did not want to run into anyone we knew. I did not want to give the rumor mill anything to churn about! He agreed. We were two friends having lunch and that was all.

As I arrived at the restaurant, the sun was shining brightly, and it was a beautiful day. I hoped he selected a seat outside. I walked slowly through the restaurant in search of my lunch companion. I did not see him. He texted and said he had arrived so that must have meant that he was seated outside. As I exited the main dining room and stepped onto the patio, I saw him. The scene was beautiful and the perfect setting for…an outing.

There was a colorful waterfall that provided a soft melody of rushing waters. The patio was adorned with umbrella covered tables that allowed a small kiss from the warm sun. Soft music was playing in the background and the smell of amazing cuisine hung on every wave of air that floated by. As I said, the scene was perfect. There was Clark, smiling from ear to ear.

We sat and talked. He complimented me on my dress. I downplayed the outfit. Yes, it took me over an hour of clothes changing to pick this one, but he did not need to know that. I thanked him for the compliment. After ordering appetizers we began to get caught up on our journeys over the past sixty days. He shared about his experience in Texas and that he realized that he was not supposed to be there. I tried to hide my enthusiasm because him not being there did not mean he planned on being here – being with me.

As we enjoyed lunch, the conversation became somewhat flirtatious. He talked about the phone call when I was in Texas at the conference. He talked about a pair of jeans that I wore to a meeting several months ago. The interesting thing about the jeans is that they were my favorite jeans and I had not worn them in 6 years. Of course, a logical person would have gotten rid of them, but they were my favorite jeans and I could fit them again! Those jeans brought sexy back. The other interesting thing about the jean day is, that was the day when I saw him differently. He was more playful and relaxed. He was having fun and engaged in the discussion. On that day he smiled.

I was now learning that on that day he saw me differently too. Wow!

He said that he was involved at the time, so he could do nothing about what he saw, but now he was not involved. He looked at me as if it was my turn to make an important move. I looked at him with a blank stare and smiled. I was not going to let him off the hook that easy. If he had something to say, he'd better start talking. I was a good listener. Of course, he already knew that.

He continued to drop hints, yet never said that he wanted to date me. He even said, "Since you asked me out on this date, what did you have in mind?" I interjected, "Wait a minute! Ask you out on a date? When did I ask you out on a date? I asked you to lunch to thank you, but if in your mind this was a date, we should explore that concept." He looked at me and laughed, "Oh, so that is your story?" I replied with a big smile, "Yes and I am sticking to it." We both laughed.

Was I ready to date? What would that mean? I have accepted that I am not moving to Arizona. Is this what is next for me? Then reality hit. The voice in my head began to sound the alarm. "You cannot do this – you have leukemia!" For a moment, I had forgotten, again.

I then began to share my journey. I told him about my last week in Arizona and receiving the reminder call for my annual physical. I talked to him about my D-Day call. I even shed light on the week of the biopsy and all that he encountered unaware. I held back my tears and tried to not sound sad. As I finished explaining the timeline of my new normal, I looked him in the eye and said, "That is why this is not a date. I would not get anyone tangled in the mess that is my life. I am doing my best to remain positive and hold it together. I would not want to be a burden on anyone."

He looked me in the eye and took my hand and said, "You know we can get through this together. I can handle this."

His words took my breath away. What was my friend saying? Was he saying that he wanted to date me? More importantly, that he was willing to date me despite the diagnosis? I did not know what to say. I was silenced by his kindness and shocked by his loving nature. He demonstrated the epitome of LIVE LOVE to me.

We continued the conversation and enjoyed a delectable lunch. Neither of us wanted the lunch to end, so we decided to go to the park and walk along the lake. The scenery was gorgeous. We began at the yacht club and watched the boats ride the wave. As we sat on the bench, he tried to put his arm around me. I purposely did not sit close enough for that to happen. I was not ready for that. We walked down to the beach and tossed rocks. We competed to see who could skip more waves. I think I won that competition. (We will go with that assumption.) We then walked along the path. There were beautiful flowers, friendly walkers, energized dogs, and joy. He and I shared an experience of joy. At that moment, I grabbed his hand. We walked hand in hand and discussed the beauty all around. The park had an actual ship anchor in the yard. We both took pictures by the anchor. We then discussed what the anchor symbolized for each of us. The conversations were easy and continuous. We laughed and talked about music – our common love and personal soundtracks. The day felt magical. It felt right. As we walked to the cars to end the evening, I began to get worried.

What was going to happen next? Would we shake hands or high five? Was a hug appropriate or would there be more? As we approached the cars, I became anxious and very nervous. He asked if I was ok. I lied and told him everything was fine. He would soon learn the truth. What happened next was unimaginable. I have never been so embarrassed.

STRONG WILL

Our cars were parked side by side. There was about three feet of space between them. When we arrived at the cars, Clark stepped down off the curb and sat on the hood of his car. Now it was my turn. But wait, how should I step down? If I step with my back to him, that would cause us to be close and almost spooning. If I step off the curb facing him, my womanhood would nearly be pressed against him. What was I supposed to do?

I decided that I would step down in such a way, my side and shoulder would be facing him. That was not suggestive nor was that too intimate. That was my plan. Unfortunately, as I stood on the very high curb and thoroughly designed my strategy, my feet became tangled in the very important dress I chose to wear on this day. Then it happened.

I lunged off the curb, but my feet did not move. My shoe had come off and both feet were entangled in the bottom of my dress. I was falling. No, I was not stumbling or tripping. I was about to fall face flat on the concrete. How could this be happening? Clark jumped up and caught me.

Before you paint this beautifully romantic picture in your head, let me stop you. That is not what happened. I landed with my face buried in his chest. He caught me by the arms which caused them to be up like chicken wings. And yes, my feet were still on the curb! This man saved my life! I was falling and had no way to catch myself or reduce the likelihood of injury.

I was so embarrassed, I could have fainted! He calmly asked, "Are you ok?" I replied, "I think so." We were having this conversation in the position I just described.

He then asked, "When I stand you up, are you going to jump in your car and leave?" I felt obligated to be honest, "Yes, absolutely. As soon as you stand me up, I am going to put my shoe back on, straighten out my dress, and go home." The conversation did not end there. He asked, "But what if I wanted you to fall into my arms? What if I willed you to this?"

I did not care if he wished upon a star, rubbed a magic lamp, or pushed me himself! I was so unbelievably embarrassed it took everything I had to not break into tears.

I then began a self-pep talk, "Listen, everyone has moments of embarrassment. It happens. You must get past this. We are going to be ok." Mind you, I was having this conversation out loud- face in chest, arms in the chicken wing hold.

He interrupted and said, "I do not mean to interrupt you, but I am going to stand you up now." He stood me up and before I could utter another word, he kissed me. Clark, my friend, kissed me. And that is how we ended our first date.

There is no way for a person to control everything in their life. If you are anything like me, you sometimes forget. Well, life has a way of reminding you. Overthinking is a bad habit. It removes you from being present and moves you to the role of orchestrating. It is ok to let go and go with the flow. Do it by choice before life chooses for you!

I went from tripping over myself to becoming head over heels. This new development was a pleasant surprise. We talked daily and had already decided we would have a second date. He wanted to take me out for my birthday. I accepted. Two dates in five days, this was getting interesting.

We enjoyed a memorable evening that included an ice cream Sunday adorned with a birthday candle. It was a happy birthday indeed. I was alive, happy, and Clark caught me as I was falling.

OFF THE GRID

We were officially dating. We were a couple and each day brought new discoveries. We discussed our interests, histories, and failures. We agreed to keep our relationship protected, so we took special care to find locations that allowed us to have privacy. It was an incredible adventure. I was introduced to parts of the community that I did not know existed. I ate meals at fabulous restaurants. We walked through beautiful parks and lake front communities. We even drove down scenic roads that provided all the sights and sounds of a beautiful summer in Wisconsin.

I believed him. He could handle my circumstance. I felt like I could climb the tallest mountain with this man. He would guide me, catch me, pull me up, and be by my side the entire time. In my spirit I heard, "We got this!"

Although my joy grew, I was constantly reminded of other realities. I began to experience one symptom of Leukemia – fatigue. On most days I was full of energy and prepared to run a marathon, but once a week I would hit a wall. I would be fatigued. The only solution was for me to rest. This feeling of bottoming out was a stark difference from my normal active day. Clark noticed. He asked lots of questions. Then something changed. When it was time to go out, he would ask, "Do you want to stay home?" Of course not, it was summer, and I planned to enjoy it. He also questioned, "How are you feeling? Is everything ok?" When I told him I was ok, he would often follow up with, "Are you sure?"

I did not like this feeling. What was his problem? Why was he acting like this? Why was he treating me like something was wrong? We had to have a conversation. I asked him to come over and we would stay inside. I was prepared to tell him good-bye. That conversation could not take place in public. It would be better to have that discussion in the privacy of my home.

The evening began pleasantly. We had small talk about the weather and the day, but then he began the inquisition. "How are you feeling? Did you eat today? Did you take your medicine?" I interrupted him. He knew I was angry. I did not try to hide it. I asked him to leave. He had only been there for twenty minutes, but I wanted him to go. He obliged but asked, "Can I call you later?" I mumbled in disgust, "Sure." I did not want to have the discussion in anger, but we needed to talk. I decided to tell him when he called later. Maybe it would be easier over the phone.

When he called that evening he asked, "What did I do?" He sounded sincerely concerned and confused. He disarmed my anger and forced me to take a step back to properly categorize his behavior. I took a deep breath and asked, "What is your biggest fear?" He responded, "Rejection." He began to explain traumatic experiences in past relationships that hurt him to the core. He could not stand rejection.

I thought, "I bet this evening was a joy then." After hearing his answer, I apologized for asking him to leave earlier. I continued, "Do you know what my biggest fear is? Pity. I do not ever want anyone to treat me like I am helpless, hopeless, or pitiful. And right now, that includes, treating me like I am sick! That behavior comes from a place of defeat and throwing in the towel. It is a look that says – you poor thing. I hate that, and I do not want anyone around me who chooses to interact that way. I will not tolerate it!"

I continued, "I am not sick. I have a situation and am going through a circumstance. That is all!" Clark sat in silence for what seemed like forever. My hands were shaking, and tears were rolling down my face. I was angry, disappointed, and hurt all at the same time. I knew that he was showing that he cared and was genuinely concerned. That did not matter to me. I needed to know that he did not see me as the girl that was dying. I could not stomach the thought of that being his image of me.

He eventually spoke in a soft, apologetic voice, "I am so sorry. Please forgive me. You are right, and I will never do that again."

The ice melted off my heart. The protective wall of bricks fell around me. I was open to remaining in this new endeavor with him. He was sorry, and I was as well. We continued our conversation that evening. We began a new chapter in our exploration. We became closer. We shared our concerns, embarrassments, and the kryptonite that Superman did not want anyone to know existed. His secret was safe with me, and I finally found a place where I too was safe. He had me. I was safe with him.

DECLUTTER

While visiting one day, Clark asked about my plans for the boxes in the garage. I asked him if he was willing to take them into the basement for me. He agreed. As he moved the boxes into the basement, we discussed how our lives were so carefully planned out. We talked about how we were both moving to our dream destinations and starting something new.

We talked about the larger plan that does not need our permission. The divine plan that knows what is around the corner and provides what is needed to take care of us. We laughed, I told him, "See, if you were still in Texas, you would not be here to help me move my belongings into the basement."

He asked, "So what is your plan after I move these boxes into the basement. What are you going to do next?" I told him of my garage conversation with God at the beginning of the summer, "God said my life needed to be decluttered to make room for something new."

As I heard the words that were coming out of my mouth, it suddenly had meaning. I understood. Was Clark the something new God spoke about? Only time would tell, but for now, the basement had plenty of space and Clark's back was strong enough for my in-house relocation plan. It was journey day 255 and the decluttering had begun.

✏ MARKER MESSAGE

My elementary school teacher used to say, "One's attitude determines their altitude!" The truth is, people can make anywhere their home. You must however make the necessary adjustments to survive there. If you live in a cold climate, you must have proper outer wear. If you live in a hot climate, your coverings must be breathable and protect you from the elements. Families in Alaska live six months in the darkness and six months in continual light. The point is, we must adjust. The biggest adjustment is your attitude. Regardless of what is happening, YOU determine if you are sitting high and swinging your legs or sitting low and looking up to see the bottom. You must decide.

THINGS ARE LOOKING UP

MARKERS OF JOY

I. You have history.

The problems you are facing are not the first set of difficulties you have encountered. Do not jump off the ledge. Take your time and process. Let your history be your guide.

    A. In sports, teams review their game footage to learn how to be better. They look at their plays and identify weaknesses in their plans. They analyze where they created gaps that cost them the win. They see if players were out of position. They also examine if the plays were executed properly. The review allows direction on what needs to be done differently. Review the footage

MARKER MESSAGE

of past circumstances in your life. What will you do differently this time?

B. While examining the game footage, teams also look at the opposing team. What can be learned about them that will help in the next face-off? Where are they strongest and what weaknesses are exposed? As you prepare to address your current issue, what do you know about your opposer? Have you completed proper research? Do you know anyone who has experienced this same battle or something similar? Do not go into the battle blind. Watch the game film!

II. Wait for the finale.

There are times when we move and act too soon. We get a slight glimpse of trouble and we either fall apart or begin the battle. There are some circumstances that are allowed to encounter your life to make you better. All those encounters are not going to feel like reasons to throw a party.

A. "And we know that all things work together for good to them that love God, to them who are called according to his purpose." Romans 8:28 KJV

B. You must believe that something good is going to happen in the end. It will be good for you in the end. You owe it to yourself to wait it out. Do not walk out the theater before seeing the end of the movie. Your life is not like the life of anyone else. Their script is not yours. Just wait.

C. Stay focused on purpose. There is a reason for what you are experiencing. The purpose may be

MARKER MESSAGE

intimate and quite personal, or it may be for someone else to experience through you. Regardless of the vehicle, it is yours to drive. Walk in purpose on purpose. Focus your gaze on where you want to be. Let purpose be your beacon to the correct path to follow. What could be the purpose of my current circumstance?

III. Be present.

I read a quote from Buddha that stated, "The secret of health for both mind and body is not to mourn for the past, worry about the future, or anticipate troubles, but to live in the present moment wisely and earnestly." (Wachob, J. 2010) Are you living in the present? If not, how about starting now?

CHAPTER 5
BEING BELOW BOTTOM

Bad things happen to good people…and then life gets even worse! Now what?

Paulo Coelho, author of The Alchemist, said, "Life has many ways of testing a person's will, either by having nothing happen at all or by having everything happen all at once." (Anderson, A.R. 2015).

WELCOME BACK

Now that life seemed to stabilize, it was time to begin a new contract. I missed being at work and my hiatus had served me well. I would begin my new contract after Labor Day. This adventure would allow me to visit Nebraska. As we discussed the details and began working on the negotiations, I felt renewed. I was confident about my future. Hitting rock bottom was a distant memory. I had even come to grips with my new normal. I was moving forward, despite all that I had experienced. I also realized that I was in love. Not, with a job. No, I was in love with myself, my life, and the man who wanted to be a part of them both.

The financial reality of being an entrepreneur is the need to keep adequate cash flow. I was financially stable, but also needed to handle the medical bills associated with my new condition. This upcoming contract would be the boost I needed to help pay my medical bills without depleting my savings account.

The medical industry is interesting to me. I applaud the expertise of doctors and those who take care of a person during illness. They are heroes in my eyes. The industry, however, can be frustrating and confusing. Medical bills are the leading cause of this dynamic of irritation. When a person is ill, you are at the mercy of the door you walk through. There are not the same types of choices that exist in other parts of life. You make one choice and the remainder of the journey is out of your control. You first decide, I do not want to continue with the current condition and I need medical attention to make the change. This of course, is a wise choice and hopefully one that is not made too late. Then there is a sort of free fall that occurs afterwards.

I believe there is a better way for the medical industry to work with those in need of care. Allow me to share my dreams of better:

What if the medical attention came with a menu. What if there were options to my charges. Could I select a basic procedure versus a premium experience? For example, when I am choosing medication, if the results are the same, I choose generic if it is cheaper. I asked myself, are there other generic options available beyond the medication area?

Someone decides the hourly rate for my doctor, nurse, urologist, anesthesiologist, and lab tests. I participate unaware and hoping for the best. There is no flat fee for a doctor. There can be two specialists at the same hospital seeing patients, one patient will pay X and the other will pay X plus 10. Why must my life be an algebra problem?

My dream of better puts all the costs up front and allows the patient to be informed and even decide if another option exists. Can someone run a price check before we begin?

This experience made me realize how much control I did

not have on the financial impact my condition would have on my life. It is not a criticism of the system, it is merely my observation and surrender! I have no crystal ball or preview of the bills heading my way. I need the service and will pay whatever it costs, somehow. Who knows? Welcome back dear friend – that darn uncertainty has returned to the building!

WHOSE PLAN

I was not stressing about my bills because my new contract was going to be secured soon, at least I thought. Then again, I have been wrong before!

I received a call from my contact who informed me that the contract was being placed on hold. The organization found a previous employee that would return and help stabilize everything. I was happy for them, but disappointed as well. Did they not know I had bills to pay?

Although I wanted the contract, I trusted that there was a divine reason for the change of circumstances. At this point, I developed a level of trust for divine intervention. If a plan is aborted, I believe that either something better is coming, or I dodged a situation. Either way, I am ok with change. The plan is not mine anyway. I trust God! I am eager to see where this journey is about to lead.

Allen Saunders was quoted as saying, "Life is what happens to us while we are making other plans." (Copquin, C.G. 2012)

I now had time to experience more of my life, while I was in between contracts.

IN BETWEEN

Although I felt healthy, I noticed the return of the migraine. It had been many weeks since the last episode, but the headache was back with the same intensity as before. The initial migraine came after I had my biopsy. That was in July. Last time, the headache lasted seven days. This was a month later. It was the end of August and I had a busy week of meetings, but I can endure seven days. I did it before! I had a scheduled doctor's appointment that week, so I would inform him of the migraine return if I was still in pain.

As with most migraines I was nauseous, could not tolerate sound, or brightness. I apologized a lot that week. I attended meetings with sunglasses on, requested that people lower their voices, and looked seasick most of the day. Fortunately, people were sympathetic and thanked me for keeping the appointments instead of staying in bed. Honestly, I was in too much pain to lay down. Keeping active was my choice to try to ignore the pain. Although, that plan was not working out as well as I had hoped.

On Thursday I visited my doctor. I did not give him the chance to ask how I was doing. I said quickly, "Doctor, my head is hurting so bad. You must prescribe me something. The pain killer I am taking is not even taking the edge off. It is as if I am eating candy, without the sweet taste!"

This was my sixth day and I figured with a little help from the doctor, I could make it through day seven and all would be well. I left my doctor's visit feeling hopeful. My Leukemia results were heading in the right direction and I had a prescription to address this migraine. I felt very pleased.

I began the prescription immediately, but I figured it needed time to work through my system. By midday Friday, the pain had lessened but was still present. I was able to rest that evening. My plan was to sleep away the pain. When the morning sun creeped through my window, I would be facing day eight and the migraine would be no more. Good night pain, good night.

I woke up early Saturday morning. The sun was bright, yet my eyes did not hurt. The birds were chirping, and I enjoyed the sound. Could it be? Is the migraine over? I leaped from the bed, excited about the release from the prison of pain. As I stood to my feet it happened – pounding! My head was pounding as if a drummer had moved into my body. I thought, "How could this be? This is day eight. What is going on here?" I did not have time for this today. I had promised my aunt a ride to the airport. She was visiting family which was 45 minutes away. I had to keep this commitment. My aunt was visiting from Texas and very serious flooding was occurring. She had to return to take care of her home. It was the weekend before Labor Day, and she had a flight to catch. There was no time for a migraine.

I kept my commitment. As we rode, I talked to her about the recurring migraine. My aunt suggested I contact my doctor and give him an update. After speaking with her, I realized that I neglected to tell my doctor that the headache had been present for seven days. I am not sure if that came up in the conversation.

After dropping off my aunt, I returned home with my headache. It had been days since I completed a mindfulness walk. I decided to go for a walk. I thought that maybe increasing the blood flow throughout my entire body would help reduce the pressure in my head. So, I walked. I completed a four-mile journey which felt amazing. I saw two rabbits, watched a bird and squirrel quarrel, and enjoyed the smell of fragrant flowers along my path. The sweat felt refreshing. The sun on my skin felt like a warm hug.

Unfortunately, the migraine remained. Maybe a nap will

help.

As I laid down on the couch, I felt a rush of heat all over my face. My sinuses were burning, my eye socket felt dry and my face was on fire! Ok, clearly a nap is not going to happen. It is time to go to the hospital and get a different prescription for this migraine! I jumped in my car, so I could drive to the hospital. The pain was intensifying, and I could not delay any longer. As I pulled out of the garage, it began to rain. It began to storm. The skies were dark, the trees were blowing, and the rain was blinding. I could barely see with the storm and the pain I was experiencing. I never left the driveway. Where did this storm come from? It was sunny and clear during my walk and now this? I called a friend and asked her to assist, "Hello, what are you doing?" She replied, "Nothing what is going on?" I did not want to alarm her, so I asked, "Can you give me a lift? I know it is raining, but I cannot drive right now." She sounded puzzled, "O.K. no problem, where do you need to go?" I was relieved she said yes. "I need to go to the emergency room. My head is still hurting, and I need something strong to make it stop." She arrived at my house within 5 minutes. I am convinced that she ran multiple red lights, but I will not judge her. She was helping a friend in need, and I was truly in need!

The emergency room was quiet, even though it was a holiday weekend. I was grateful for the fast service. That evening, I worked with an emergency room doctor and a resident. The initial diagnosis revealed that I was dehydrated. They began fluids immediately. After 15 minutes the pain seemed to intensify. The doctors tried multiple medications to address the pain. After each dose, my pain seemed to increase. I finally asked, "You do know the goal is to eliminate this pain, right? Because whatever you are doing is moving in the wrong direction!" I was not attempting to be a difficult patient, I just needed to be sure we were working from the same plan.

The doctor decided a scan would be appropriate. There had to be a logical explanation for this migraine's intensity. After the scan, the resident came in to ask a few questions. She asked my friend to leave. As I reflect on the experience, my pain and the meds were not making the job easy for the resident. She asked three questions. "Have you fallen recently? Have you bumped your head? Is there a situation occurring?" I was able to answer the first two questions quickly. I had not fallen or bumped my head. But the situation? I was not sure what she was referring to. Maybe she meant my Leukemia. Because of my assumption, the conversation took a turn for the worst. We were having two different conversations. I was discussing life with Leukemia and I was not sure of her topic at all.

I said, "Yes, there is a situation. I have Leukemia. It has been stressful. I have been in stressful times before, it has never resulted in this. This migraine is unbearable." As the conversation continued about stress, support, home life, and safety, I was not sure where she was heading. The emergency doctor returned and asked her if we were done. She shrugged her shoulders. At this point I realized that the confusing conversation had a purpose, which we did not achieve. The doctor asked, "Ma'am has someone been hitting you or causing you to hit your head?"

I was flabbergasted by his question. I responded, "Are you asking me if I am being abused? Do you see two people in here? Are you serious?" His question hit a nerve because in my teen years, I had experienced a violent dating relationship that I hid from everyone. I promised myself that I would never let another person harm me like that again.

He apologized and explained that in situations like this,

the hospital is required to ask. "Wait, situation like this?" I asked. At this point, my friend returned into the room. She gave me a strange look as she heard the exchange.

He looked at the resident with a look of disgust. Apparently, there was something else on the agenda for our little chat that did not get accomplished. He walked closer to the bed and began speaking in a slow and soft voice. "Ma'am, your scan revealed two concerning masses. You have a subdural hematoma."

I did not know what that meant. "Exactly what is that? What do I have?" I asked. I was not ready to handle yet another disease attacking my body right now! He held my hand and said, "your brain is bleeding, and the neurosurgeon is on the way."

I looked at my friend and said, "Call my momma!"

As a little girl, I grew up on the west side of Chicago. I experienced alleys and gangways. I saw my share of danger and I knew to walk the other way. One thing that I was sure of, if things ever got out of hand, I just had to make one call. I knew this would be the ultimate problem solver, conflict ender, craziness halter, business handler – MY MOMMA.

Now, when this horrific news was being shared with me, all I could do was request the call that would make everything better. Call My Momma!

After ensuring the important call was completed, I looked back at the doctor and asked, "So this is not a migraine?"

For seven days prior to today, I had convinced myself that I knew what was wrong. Although I did not have the solution, I was certain of my diagnosis. I had spent the entire week describing the debilitating force of my migraine. I talked with great confidence. I knew what this was. I just needed help making it end. I am now being told, I am wrong? I cannot wrap my mind around this new development!

The doctor shook his head no, "Your head is hurting, but this is something more serious than that. A subdural hematoma is the name for bleeding in the cavity between the skull and brain."

At that point, I laid my head down and let the tears flow down my cheeks. This is worse than I thought. What next? I do not have a plan for this. I began to talk to God...

"Lord, I thought things were looking up. As I began to embrace the joy, peace, and love that I was experiencing, I misunderstood the direction of my journey. I had fallen even further than before. There are approximately 2,000 steps in one mile. If leaving the job was my bottom, I have officially landed One Mile Below Bottom! Now I see why I could not go to Nebraska, but really, my brain is bleeding?"

At that moment, the neurosurgeon entered the room. He began to explain that the scan showed that I had two points of bleeding. One point was older than the other. He asked if I had this pain before now. "Yes, I had this migraine a little over four weeks ago and then it came back."

Although the conversation was serious and scary, he brought a sense of humor that made me feel better.
He said, "Yes, I saw that there was a significant time between the two bleeds. I need to share a few things with you. First, let's stop calling this a migraine. This is not a migraine. Secondly, moving forward, I want you to know the difference between a headache and a rip in between your brain and skull. Can you do that for me?" I smiled and said yes. To which he replied, "Good, you seemed like a smart lady."

The doctor left the room and promised to return shortly. My mom had been updated on everything he said. She told my friend to tell me, "I am on the way." Although my mother was not a doctor and this experience would be new for both of us, knowing she was coming made me feel better. This was more than I was ready to face alone.

I was attempting to process what this meant. Have I been bleeding all these weeks? What if I had died in my sleep? What if I had fallen out on my walk today? Or behind the wheel with my aunt in the car? I realized that I had been protected from tragedy and was blessed to be alive.

The doctor returned to the room. He informed me that emergency surgery was required and that he had done these many times before. As the tears rolled down my cheeks again, he took my hand, looked me in the eyes and said, "I am the best, you are going to be fine." Using the most commanding voice I could pull out, I informed him that my mom was on her way, so we had to wait until she arrived.

He asked, "Ok what side of town is she coming from?" I shyly replied, "Kansas City." He looked at me and smiled, "Did I neglect to mention that this was an emergency procedure?" At this point, I could not find the humor. I began to cry for real. I sobbed and could barely breath. My friend hugged me and began making calls. I was in trouble.

After reading my chart, the doctor informed me that my surgery would be first thing in the morning. I had to be transferred to the main hospital and I was scheduled for the first slot. I remember asking if my friend should take me or would they give me a ride. I believe I was in shock and was not thinking clearly. I realized at this point, my neurosurgeon was kind, patient, and had a sense of humor. He replied, "Thank you for the carpool concept, but we are going to send you in an ambulance just to be sure you do not get lost or stop off for a burger."

I hugged my friend and told her thank you. She did what

any big sister would do. She kissed my forehead and told me she would see me at the hospital. When I arrived at the hospital, they checked me into the intensive care unit for the night. I remember being visited by several of my Sister-Friends that night. I felt loved. The remainder of the night was a blur. On Journey day 268, I found out – it was not a migraine!

ONE SUNDAY MORNING

I slept through the night and was awoken by my surgeon. He asked me if I was ready. I replied, "The question is, are you ready?" We both laughed and prepared to head down to the pre-op room. As they wheeled me into the room, my Pastors were present along with my Sister-Friends. Clark and I were keeping our relationship a secret, so he was aware, but could not come. The group prayed, and they told me everything would be fine. I agreed with them. I was no longer afraid. It was in God's hands at this point.

Before surgery, my neurosurgeon explained the procedure and discussed a few post-operation conditions that could occur (slurred speech, hand weakness, distorted vision). Because this was brain surgery, there were possible side effects of the procedure that I needed to understand. I had internal peace as he explained the process to me. The procedure required two incisions into my skull. There would be the insertion of a cushion material to pad my brain as it returned to its natural position after the removal of fluid and reduction of swelling. He would mend the rips, stop the bleeding and sew me up. Pretty simple. I was ready, but I had one final question. "Can you promise me that when you are done, this pain will end? I want to stop counting. Today is day nine, let's not make it 10!" He promised, and I closed my eyes.

The next voice I heard was my neurosurgeon. Did he have

something else to discuss? We needed to get this procedure under way. I am ready, we can talk later.

He said, "We are done. Everything went well." I was confused. He completed the surgery? I immediately thought of the side effects. What do I need to deal with now? He continued to explain, "I know I told you of the steps in the procedure. There seemed to be a different plan."

I took a deep breath. Was he about to share bad news? Was he not able to do everything he hoped to do? What now?

He explained, "I opened your head as I said I would, but then your body took over. The fluids excreted themselves, the swelling flattened, and your brain popped back into place. I did not touch a thing!"

The tears began to flow, and I said, "That was God." He replied, "Indeed." I had a voice. I could see. My hands were strong, and God completed my surgery himself! I may be One Mile Below Bottom, but my God is here with me!

My surgeon continued, "As far as I am concerned, you can go home." It was good to see he had not lost his sense of humor. I looked at him and replied, "Since you were in my head a few hours ago, I am going to hang around for a few days if you do not mind." We both laughed, and I went back to sleep knowing that day 10 would not arrive. My 'migraine' was no more!

SHE MADE IT

While napping in my room in ICU, my mother arrived. She came in the room and gave me a kiss on my forehead. I smiled and told her, "I tried to wait for you, but I lost that fight." We both laughed. She sat down and shared with me her adventure as she attempted to get to me.

When she received the phone call last night, she immediately jumped in her car and was prepared to drive. After buckling her seat belt, she looked in the passenger seat and realized what was happening. She had jumped out of bed, in her pajamas, grabbed her pit bull and ran to the car. There she sat in her pajamas with her dog ready to go. After she thought the plan through she realized that another approach was needed. She disconnected both of their seat belts and went back into the house. She called the airline and booked a flight for the next morning. Her adventure did not end there. Because she did not rest the night before, she was alarmed when she woke up on the airplane in Washington DC. When booking her flight, she did not pay attention to the detail of the flight path. She asked for the ticket on the flight that would get her to Wisconsin first. She neglected to note the zig zag flight path used to get her there. By the time my mom arrived, she wanted to climb in the bed with me. She had earned the right to do it too. Now that my mom was there, we could both get a little rest.

SUPERMAN PRAYS

My mother became reacquainted with my friend Clark during this ordeal. My visiting times were restricted. There were times no one was allowed in the room. My mom would go for walks, run errands, and make phone calls. On some of the breaks, my mom would sit and talk with Clark. If he arrived at the hospital and could not see me, he would sit in the waiting room and pray. He prayed for my healing. He prayed for my comfort. He prayed for my health. He prayed with and for my mom.

Clark had already won my heart, but he now had my mom's too. She met the man who she believed would take care of her baby. A man who knew what to do in the time of crisis.

She met my Superman. He could not personally fix my situation, but he did not run either. He was committed to the process, and for that I knew my future included him – regardless of what else the future held.

My visiting time with him at the hospital was cut short due to other people visiting. I was excited to see them, but I still wanted to keep our relationship private. This was nearly impossible at the hospital. When Clark came to visit, and could see me, I had my mom run interference and not let anyone else visit during this time. The hospital staff helped too. They allowed me to restrict visiting as I saw fit.

It was great to feel supported and loved as I recovered from surgery. The doctor kept his promise. My head no longer hurt. I had received 21 staples and a new haircut. I was so happy to be rid of pain that I did not mind. Also, I was happy to be alive. So, a new look seemed like a gift that I accepted with open arms.

THE SUN SHINED

My recovery had moments of difficulty due to my inability to accept some of the medications administered. I spent time vomiting and having horrible bone pain related to my Leukemia. I had stopped chemotherapy although my body was still under attack. My recovery days were difficult, but I was determined to stabilize so I could go home.

I woke up Wednesday morning and noticed the sun peeking through the blinds. I had not noticed the sun on any other day. I was preoccupied by other matters. But on this day, I was ready to face the world. The doctor told me that I would be released later in the day and I was overjoyed by the news. I asked my mother to open the blinds. She opened to let the sun in the room, but what I received was even more magnificent.

I had not looked out the window. I knew where I was but did not really have a mental picture of the location. The opening of the blinds revealed the most beautiful site. Outside the window was a view that looked like paradise. There was a beautiful view of Lake Michigan. There were three white yachts on the water cruising by, causing a slight ripple in the current. The winds were slow as the waves barely showed any peaks. In the lakefront park people were walking dogs, throwing frisbees, and riding bikes. My mom opened the window and I beheld a spiritual message I almost forgot – LIVE LOVE. I had survived. I was alive. There was a beautiful world outside that window waiting to welcome me back home. Yes, it was time for me to leave the hospital and go home. I was ready.

SHE IS BACK, AGAIN

It was great to be home. This time was different. If I had yelled, "Honey I am home!" the feeling would have not been as before. My mother was there, my brother had come to town, and I had a sweetie in my life. I was no longer alone. There was a welcome committee waiting for me!

The doctor placed me on bed rest for a few days. I felt like a prisoner. I could only walk from my bed to the bathroom and back. My steps were slow and steady, but I felt a bit unsure. I had no choice but to be obedient. My bedroom is upstairs in the house and I was not ready to tackle stairs. Bed rest it is, for now.

When you experience something this extreme you will never forget it, but you also do not truly comprehend all the details of the experience while it is happening. I decided that I wanted photos to capture the moment. I had a friend come and take my pictures. I did not want to miss the beauty of the experience. My scars tell my story of the miraculous. My tears of joy deserved to be preserved for future use. This experience will remind me of God's love for me. I know I am loved because of everything that did not happen!

When preparing for my pictures, I was trying to figure out how to style my hair. My scalp was still sensitive from the surgery earlier that week. But I was also reaching the point of stir crazy. Preparing for the photo shoot gave me something to focus on. As I played in the mirror, I noticed a familiar look. I looked like the Bride of Frankenstein. I have a natural grey streak in the front. When you add the 21 staples adorning the side of my now bald head, I was a modern day She-Frank! This humored me and made looking at my scars easier. What was captured that day on film will serve as my reminder of the depths I survived.

GOING SOMEWHERE

It was one week since my arrival to the emergency room. A week ago, I thought I had a migraine. I wondered, if I had known what was happening, would I have done anything differently. Looking back, it was best that everything happened so quickly. There was no time to worry, be depressed, or play the "what if" game. I am grateful for the speed of the miracle experience.

I had survived my days of bed rest. I completed a photoshoot to memorialize the experience. I met a new alter ego, thanks to my hair. I was now ready to move on. I was no longer sick. This too shall pass. As I headed to bed Saturday night, I was determined for Sunday to begin my new week. I had a plan.

After breakfast Sunday morning, I told my mom that I was going to take a shower and did not need her help. She hesitated but entertained my request. "I know you do not like people treating you like you are helpless. Just be careful. Move slowly and do not try to do too much." I promised, and she left me alone to bathe in peace.

It was time to unleash my plan. I showered but did not get back into bed as my daily routine had become. I put on a dress, applied my makeup, and styled my hair. It felt as if I had accomplished a major feat however my plan was not yet complete. There was one last step required.

From my bedroom I slowly walked to the hall stairs. I carefully sat at the top of the stairs. One step at a time, I scooted down the stairs on my bottom. I continued until I made it to the bottom of the stairwell. My mom met me at the bottom, "And where do you think you are going?"

I replied, "I cannot stay in that room one more day. I am coming to sit on the couch. I had surgery a week ago and I am no longer sick. This is a new week and I am ready to live it."

She laughed and replied, "That is fine, but if you reach for those car keys I am calling your Pastor, Bishop Burt, and he will deal with you!" That was funny. She knew how much I loved my Pastor and regarded him as my father figure. There would be no need to bother him. The couch was my goal and I felt proud – mission accomplished.

After accomplishing my great escape, my mother and I had an enjoyable Sunday afternoon. I spent most of the day napping, but I felt free and stronger since leaving out of the room.

My mom used the opportunity to clear the room and

refresh the bedding. A perspective was revealed to me while she was in the room. I remembered the Bible story of a man healed at the pool of Bethesda (John 5:1-9 NIV). In the story, there was a pool that had healing powers once "troubled" by the angels. However, only the first person in the pool received healing. There was a man who had been waiting by the pool for thirty-eight years. During an encounter with Jesus, the man was told to pick up his bed and walk. He did not have to wait for the angel to stir the water. He was experiencing a miraculous healing and told to walk by faith.

I thought to myself, "That is what I need to do." I called my mom downstairs to hear my revelation. "Mom, I know what I need to do. I need to pick up my bed and walk." She looked at me and said, "Ok, so do you not want me to change the linen?"

It was on that day, that I decided it was time to get a new bed. The bed I had was my sick bed. It was the bed that I laid in after a long stressful day at work. It was the bed that I knelt at when I prayed to God for healing from Leukemia. It was the bed of my confinement after brain surgery. I was ready to be made whole. I was going to pick up my bed, immediately. No longer was I nursing my wounds. I was ready to let the past go. The past was necessary and provided teachable moments along my journey. I am looking to the future.

It was journey day 278. It was on that day I placed an order for a new bed. I ordered a pillow-top plush queen-sized bed. This girl is ready to leave the poolside. I am not waiting any longer. I am whole. I believe I am healed from it all! And I will have a new bed to prove it!

📏 MARKER MESSAGE

J.K. Rowling, the author of Harry Potter, stated, "Rock Bottom became the solid foundation on which I rebuilt my life." (PassItOn.com) I can relate to her sentiment. But what happens when your rock bottom is not solid? What happens when the surprises continue, and the free fall seems never ending? That is what it is like to be Below Bottom! Have you ever been there?

BEING BELOW BOTTOM

MARKERS OF JOY

I. At this point, you may be experiencing a level of tragedy that you have never faced before. You may not be able to reflect on what you did the last time this happened. There may not have been a last time.

A. Do not panic. Although this is a new experience for you, you are a survivor! Take a moment and reflect on the times you were convinced the situation you were facing was the worst possible issue you could handle.

- How did that situation work out?
- Did you learn anything from it?
- Are you still here despite it?

You are a survivor. Do not ever forget that!

B. Take time to acknowledge what is going right in your life. What are the positive attributes you are experiencing? What has not fallen apart? What brings you joy today?

- You owe it to yourself to balance the scale. We have no problem creating the detailed

MARKER MESSAGE

list of all that is wrong, disappointing, or broken. But are we giving equal time to the gifts, acts of kindness, and good things around us as well?

- Once you create your list - write it down. Share your list with someone. For another person to see you experience joy in the time of your deep pain is inspiring. It will cause them to look at small problems they complain about and realize that if YOU can overcome, they will work to do the same.

II. Affirm your next phase.

Today may be rough. Right now, may be unpleasant. This too shall pass. You must declare your next step. Speak your victory. Tell the rest of your story. You must first believe in your heart, then you must say it to ensure it is in your head.

- I will be healed.
- My marriage will be excellent.
- I will find my joy.
- I am...
- DECLARE IT AND MEAN IT!

CHAPTER 6
UPSIDE DOWN

The gift of having your world turned upside down when you are below bottom is – you are sitting <u>on top of the world</u> after the flip!

"It takes a village to raise a child," is a widely shared African Proverb. It is often quoted when discussing the current state of children. My family consists of many village prodigies. I have aunts and uncles that were never related to me by blood or marriage. They were simply friends of the family that experienced our village of love, kindness, and support. It was the village that people ran to in times of trouble or distress.

Over time, I had become independent and less reliant on the village. I had no problem being a key part of the village that gave love and support, but rarely did I lean on the village for personal needs or to be on the receiving end. I believed in the village, but my unwillingness to be vulnerable left me outside the comforts of the very village I supported.

VILLAGE IDIOT

I placed the order. Although my new bed had arrived, my walk of healing was still a work in progress. I had regained my freedom to roam the house as I pleased, but I was not able to go outside unaccompanied. To be honest, I did not feel sure of myself, so I did not mind the company. My walk was slow, and my balance was not steady. A combination of surgery, medications, and prolonged periods in bed were the cause of my current gait.

It was time for my mother to return home. She had served as my personal nurse for nearly 3 weeks. I had to set her free and allow her to live her life as well. The day before she left, she spent a significant amount of time on the phone. I thought she was managing work related matters, so I did not disturb her. I would eventually learn that she was plotting her exit, and she had a plan.

The next day, I joined Clark as he dropped my mom off at the airport. I was sad to see her leave, but I was in good hands. We returned home and spent a few hours with small talk until I became sleepy. I was prepared to walk Clark to the door when suddenly one of my Sister-Friends came by. I was not expecting any guests, so this visit was a bit odd. As Clark let her in, he kissed me on the forehead and said, "See you tomorrow."

After closing the door, I noticed that my friend had pulled out her computer, notepad, and a series of files. I looked at her in sheer confusion, "What are you doing?" She chuckled and responded, "Oh yeah, your mother worked out a schedule, I am spending the night and will be relieved in the morning."

Her plan was revealed! My mom had gathered my friends who agreed to take turns spending time with me, so I would not be home alone. I was not sure if I was infuriated or impressed. I did not like the idea of them conspiring behind my back. (Note, this was not the last time they conspired. I will tell more later). But I felt better knowing someone was in the house with me. I felt loved. I really did need my village and they were there for me, whether I liked it or not!

It is an error for a leader to think that they never need anyone. How is it that we can be there for everyone else and support all their needs, yet we feel guilty if we need help. Better yet, we feel embarrassed. And we dare not initiate a request. That is probably one of the most idiotic behaviors in my tool belt. But if I am honest, it is probably one of the oldest tools I own.

I know why and how I learned this behavior. I have heard that knowing is half the battle. Well, the other half must be something big because I was still being the village idiot!

I could barely walk 5 steps without having to grab onto something. I had a recent brain surgery. I was back on daily chemotherapy and I had convinced myself that, "I got this!" What a fool. I realized that it was time for me to stop playing the fool and get some help. If knowing truly is half the battle let me figure out what I know:

- Fear of disappointment is why I do not ask for help. If someone says yes, but then does not honor their word I am disappointed.

- Disappointment causes me to feel unworthy. I was not important enough for the person to honor their word. I of course would never ask an unreliable person, so it must be me. I am not worth it.

- Feeling unworthy makes me angry. I am angry at myself because I should be able to do it myself and then I would not need anyone else. I am angry that I even bothered anyone.

It was at the point of anger that I found the fool.

The logic journey I just described was created by a seven-year-old girl who waited for the father that never showed up. This logic was reinforced by the thirteen-year-old girl who looked in the audience in hopes that her dad would see her graduate from 8th grade. This journey was compounded by the experience of a seventeen-year-old girl lying in bed paralyzed from the neck down whose dad did not call or visit for six months because he did not want to see her like that. There was no fool. There was a disappointed little girl who leaned on the village and the chief let her fall. Listen, it was in that fall, that the tool of independence was born!

LEUKEMIA'S GIFT

When my dad and I spent time dealing with old wounds, I discussed my issues and forgave him. I, however, did not address the impact of those wounds on my character. My drive to work hard, be great, and lead a team was based upon my desire to be good enough. To be worthy. My unhealthy love affair with my job was to fill a void created by daddy issues. My insistence on being independent was the tool of my youth. I not only know how I got there, I also realized how to leave it behind. Ah, there is the other half. Welcome!

My fall below bottom showed me that I was worth it! I did not die of Leukemia. I did not suffer an aneurism in my sleep. I had friends and family willing to help me, support me, be there for me.

I had an announcement to make:

To all that willingly participate in the village that is my life. Thank you! To all that labor in secrecy to spare my feelings and side step my stupid pride – I am sorry and Thank You! To my friends who have thick enough skin to ignore me when I think I can do it alone and get mad because they do not listen to me – I love you and Thank you!

To anyone reading this book and realizing that your tool of independence has been revealed; you are not alone, just let them in.

I will no longer be a fool. I will allow others to help me and support me when I am in need. After all, it is their way of showing love. How dare I block them the opportunity to love me! The idiot has left the building!

BLEMISHED TO BLESS

My healing process was progressing, and I embraced my visits with friends. I did not allow them to continue around the clock surveillance. That only lasted for two days. I could not stand it after that. Daily visits for lunch or after work chats became my anticipated highlight. I was also cleared by the doctor to drive. My walk was stable. My balance was not an issue and I was ready to face the day. I wanted to get back to work. The leaves were beginning to turn, and the October chill was upon me. I began participating in community events to increase my exposure and prepare for my next contract.

I attended a premier for an upcoming play. Two rows in front of me, sat a man with a bald head. He caught my attention because I noticed a scar from the nape of his neck to the crown of his head. At that moment I wondered, what was his below bottom experience. And what did it take for him to find himself on top. I was fascinated by this gentleman. His disposition was positive. He was jovial during the event. He even had a smile that lit up the room. He demonstrated joy. I had to say hello.

After the reading, I walked up to him and said, "What a beautiful journey mark on your head." He smiled and replied, "I have never had anyone describe my scar like that." I smiled and said, "I have one too and it is an exclusive club." We both smiled and walked away. I felt empowered. There are others who have faced health issues and yes, their journey left a mark. Sharing the mark will help someone else know that they too can make it. His blemish blessed me. His scar spoke to my spirit. He showed me how to smile after the scar.

I decided on that day, that I would begin to share my story. Previously, I camouflaged my head and avoided discussing my surgery. I selfishly thought people would feel sorry for me. I overlooked the opportunity to inspire others with my story. It was time for the Bride of Frankenstein to meet the people. The 21 staples had been removed and I was left with my very own beautiful journey mark.

For the next 30 days, I began telling people of my healing. I began sharing my experience of favor. I shared my journey through the miraculous. I was on journey day 316 and I had found my joy in hell.

✏ MARKER MESSAGE

As a kid, I set a goal to be able to stand on my head. I practiced balancing against the wall. I would fall to the left, tumble to the right, I even found it difficult to stay against the wall. But I was determined and did not give up. Eventually, my core strengthened to the point of me being able to successfully stand on my head against the wall. Additionally, daily practice produced a product that I had not expected. One day, I was showing my mother my accomplishment, but there was not an empty wall near. So, in the middle of the floor I positioned myself and stood on my head. There was no wall there holding me up. My core handled it all. I did not even realize I could stand on my head without the wall! It took falls, repetition, and opportunity for me to learn just how strong I had become. I proudly stood on my head and enjoyed my moment of upside down!

UPSIDE DOWN

MARKERS OF JOY

I. Do not play the role of idiot.

Let the village support you. There may be experiences in your past that tell you not to trust anyone. There must be someone that is the exception to this rule. If you have not met that person yet, you now know how to spend your spare time. We were created to commune one with another. Find your village.

    A. You can survive disappointment. Do not let your fear of disappointment keep you from

---

📐 MARKER MESSAGE

---

connecting with others. Give them a chance. You may be pleasantly surprised. Be honest about your concern, but do not miss the opportunity of communal support.

B. You are worth it! If a person does let you down, it is their failure. Do not take on responsibility for the shortcomings of others. You determine your worth. Look in the mirror and repeat these words… I AM WORTH IT. You are!

C. You deserve love. Remember, one reason to allow others to support you is because it may be their way of expressing their love for you. You deserve to be loved, but you must make it possible for others to do so.

II. Beauty for Ashes – Display your journey scars and beauty marks.

There is no need to hide the trials and tribulations that shaped your life. Each leg of your journey created muscles needed for future adventures on your journey.

A. You are an overcomer. Tell your story. I believe that we have experiences, so we can pull from them when the stakes get higher. You are tested and proven strong. Because you are strong, you can endure further testing. The cycle continues, but over time you will be able to endure. Your endurance inspires others to do the same! You overcame to help others overcome. Do not miss the opportunity to share your story of being blessed. You were blessed to be a blessing to someone else.

B. Celebrate today. You may be asking why. Today

MARKER MESSAGE

is to be celebrated because it is an indication that you made it through yesterday with the opportunity to face tomorrow. It may have not been the best day ever, but you did it. Each day you experience the newest reason to celebrate - today! It is inevitable, we will all face the day of no tomorrow. Our today will become a final calling card because we will not see beyond that point. Let us not wait until that moment to be grateful for all that has passed. Celebrate today!

C. Find and keep your joy in hell! Where is your joy? What makes you smile? Are you aware that at your worst moment there is someone who has it worse off than you? You may have to retune your mind, retool your perspective, and reset your lens. Do it! There is always joy around. It is your obligation to find it. Acknowledge its presence and keep it near!

Even if you must revert to your 12-year-old self and stand on your head, enjoy your moment of upside down.

CHAPTER 7
OVERCOMING THE MILE

Yes, there are approximately 2,000 steps in a mile. If you find yourself one mile below bottom, strap your joy to your side and climb out one step at a time. I did!

REFLECTION

I may not have the answer to all the mysteries of the world. I do, however, have the answer to maintaining my joy. My joy is not for sale. It cannot be borrowed. I will not minimize it for the comfort of others. It is bright, beautiful, bold, and mine. I do not wear rose colored glasses. No, I wear the joy of the Lord and it is my covering on the hottest day. I now have a history of joy in hell, so I believe I can face whatever comes my way – with a smile. At this point, my journey was on day 533 and I planned to keep on counting!

Life may be difficult right now, but do not give up. Do not lose hope. You can overcome this. If you are a part of the village of support, share your joy with those in need. Share your story of previous trials and triumphs. Do not sit on your journey chronicles. There is someone who needs to hear your story because it is their story too, but they are afraid to learn of the ending. Spoiler alert – you win! Please let them know.

It is necessary to expect something better. One step out of the pit of pain. One moment of relief. A slight ray of sunshine on the darkest day. Expect it. Proclaim it. Declare it with your mouth and believe it in your heart. Better is yours.

Keep looking up.

My daily desire to LIVE LOVE was a quest to uncover markers of joy. This journey revealed my love of nature. I feel connected to the animals, trees, and wind. I see messages and signs all around me. They guide me and comfort me. I am not alone, but at moments when I am physically by myself, spiritual companionship is revealed. Do not miss your markers along the way. They may be simple and seem silly at times. Do not leave them unacknowledged. You will be amazed how entertaining watching a quarrel between a bird and squirrel can be. More importantly, it will help you maintain your composure when approached by the squirrel working in your office. Do not fly off the handle. Simply tweet and fly away, leaving him in the dirt.

Our earthly bodies are susceptible to various attacks that can cause your health to deteriorate. Take care of yourself. Do not ignore the signs. Go and Know. But do not lose hope for help. From the moment we are born, we are a day closer to the day we die. Today should be celebrated, but do not fear tomorrow. A negative health report is an opportunity to maximize each day. It is simply a reminder that tomorrow is not promised and none of us know the day or the hour, and all the worrying in the world cannot stop the inevitable. So why not get busy living?

THE STAIRWELL

It has been one year since my diagnosis and I now have a visualization of my journey. It has been a stairwell. Imagine a beautiful stairwell in a building with 25 or so floors. At the very top of the stairwell is a skylight that allows the sun to shine brightly through. The stairs go up and they go down. Depending on what you need, you may be on floor 4 or floor

24. The stairwell is not good or bad, it just is. Monday, you may find yourself walking down 3 flights to meet friends for lunch. Tuesday you may be climbing up 3 flights to deliver an urgent package. The stairs did not change, even if the energy you must exert did somehow increase. The stairs are the tool to get you to the floors that hold what you need.

What is the floor for you today? Be sure to adhere to all the signs:

Open with caution. Do not burst through doors of opportunity. Walk through as to be careful to not crash into what is on the other side. Take your time and enter gracefully.

No roof access. If you are trying to go to the top, why are you walking through doors that will never lead there? Stop wasting your time.

Street access. Do you know how to get totally out if you need to? Find your external exits. The day may come that you need to escape quickly. Your life may depend on it.

And finally – Share the Stair. You will need others. Even if we are not walking arm-in-arm that is fine, but please do not push or trip me along the climb.

My journey has had both ups and downs. There have been locked doors and fire extinguishers along my path. But at the end of the day, I see the sun and I am still in motion with purpose. The walls have even relayed messages of hope, peace, love, and joy as I climb! My emergency came and as instructed, I did not get on the elevator. I used the stairs and lived!

THE CONSPIRACY

I had forgiven my mother and friends for conspiring behind my back. They did so out of love. As I previously mentioned, it was not the only time they loved me in this way.

I had agreed to serve as emcee at an event hosted by my Sister-Friend entitled, Ready For Love. After a successful dress rehearsal and run through, I was excited to support her vision. She was sharing an intimate portrait of her life and her quest for love. The evening was going to be unforgettable.

After 90 minutes of jaw dropping talent, heart wrenching stanzas, and soul stirring symphonies, the event was ending. I was so proud of her. She had sacrificed her pride, privacy, and pain to help others become Ready for Love.

At rehearsal, we discussed her acknowledging her supporters and "love ambassadors." This act of kindness would close the evening for the participants.

The event was concluding, and we reached the point of acknowledgements. As we reached that moment, she changed the script. Although it was her show, she was not following the plan. She began to adlib which caused me concern. She opened the opportunity for audience participation. What was she thinking? You cannot control an open mic situation! We did not have time to give parameters and discuss the rules, but she insisted.

The first gentleman sang a beautiful love song. A couple at church had used that song in their wedding recently. It made me smile when I heard the song because I thought of their ceremony. The gentleman had a beautiful voice, so this extra insertion was successful. But it did not end there. She then asked if the audience felt ready for love. Of course, hands were raised high in the air. Because I had fully embraced my journey to LIVE LOVE, I found that moment quite enjoyable…then it happened. She called Clark and asked if he had something to say.

"Did you just call Clark? What are you doing?" I was confused and did not want to be embarrassed. I had totally lost control as emcee. As he approached the stage, all the love ambassadors that had been called to the front and acknowledged began to walk away. I followed and began to walk away as well, but everyone pushed me back to the stage.

At this point, I knew something was going on, but not quite sure what it was. Well, I quickly found out. Clark began fidgeting in his pocket and bent down. "Wait? Are you doing what I think you are doing?" I asked with slight concern in my voice. He smiled and said yes. To which I replied, "In front of all these people?" He said, "Do not be mad."

Clark asked me, in front of a crowd of 200 of our closest friends, to marry him. It was two days before valentine's day and I said yes.

Despite the diagnosis. Despite the surgery. Despite the independence. Clark wanted to spend the rest of his life with me! On this day, I had a new D-Day. Clark, AKA Dwayne, gave me a new D-Day! Dwayne and Denisha Day had begun.

LIVE LOVE

✐ MARKER MESSAGE

As I continued to develop my soundtrack of life, new songs were added based upon their message. One addition was the song Everlasting God by William Murphy. (Murphy, W. 2016). My secret to keeping my joy in hell was explained in the lyrics of his song, which became my anthem:

"The Lord is my light and salvation, whom shall I fear, whom shall I be afraid? I will wait on you. I will trust in you. I will remain confident in this, I will see the goodness of the Lord."

I learned critical lessons from the bottom. It is my hope that they will assist your climb as well.

OVERCOMING THE MILE

MARKERS OF JOY

I. Find your PURPOSE not your PLACE. There is a difference.

Your place of employment or place on a team is important but must be kept in proper perspective. There are multiple places, but one true purpose for you. As you breathe your breath and take up space daily, you are obligated to find your purpose and play your role – well. Chase purpose even if it means letting your place change for now.

II. Know when you have cracked up. We see your arm full of eggs.

It is critical for you to deal with the fragile nature of your hurts. If they have not healed, you will carry them around to stink up the place. You cannot protect all the eggs and

---

✎ MARKER MESSAGE

they will eventually crack. Before walking around with egg all over your face, heal. It is time.

III. Remember your mixed bowl of nuts. Find the humor, it is in there somewhere.

Once you have put out the fire and saved all the kittens in the tree, do not forget to laugh. Toxic stress is poison to the body and can kill you. One way to diffuse is to search for the humor in the matter. Find it and let out a gut chuckle that can ease the tension and release a bit of the stress. Practice dancing with Mr. Peanut if that helps.

IV. No Solo Climbers – We got this!

When life's issues turn into a mountain that seems impossible to move, too big to go around, and facing you as if daring you to climb it, gather a team. It is illegal to climb the infamous Mount Everest alone, due to the dangers of a solo journey. (Bhandari, R, 2017). Life is a team sport. Play it to win. Do not try to do it alone and on your own. We got this, but you must send out the invitations to achieve the WE.

V. There is a higher power with the perfect plan.

In all my effort used for planning, I have learned to pray. There is nothing wrong with devising a plan. I have learned to pray so that my plan aligns with the plan of my Father. Your experience did not catch God by surprise. Here are two scriptures that carried me through my toughest moments:

> Isaiah 43:2 (NIV)
>
> When you pass through the waters, I will be with you; And when you pass through the rivers, they will not sweep over you. When you walk

MARKER MESSAGE

through the fire, you will not be burned; The flames will not set you ablaze.

Romans 5:3-5 (NIV)
Not only so, but we also glory in our sufferings, because we know that suffering produces perseverance; perseverance character; and character hope. And hope does not put us to shame, because God's love has been poured out into our hearts through the Holy Spirit, who has been given to us.

It was no longer about counting the days beyond hitting rock bottom. It was no longer about top either. It was about life, love, and future. That day I began the count over. Now I was counting days of blessings and joy. I will not forget to LIVE LOVE. I had to journey One Mile Below Bottom, to learn to keep My Joy in Hell. He asked. I said yes. I had cancer, but it did not have me. Markers of joy pulled me out of my pit of pain. I was alive! And my newest Journey of Joy was on Day 1 and counting.

Thank you for joining me on my journey One Mile Below Bottom. It is my sincere hope that you have found inspiration to help you Keep Your Joy in Hell.

I would love to hear from you, post a comment in the Live Love Facebook Group or leave a review on Amazon:

Scan Below for the
Live Love Facebook Group

Scan Below for
Amazon Review

REFERENCES

Western Tanager. (n.d.). Field Guide to Birds of North America. Retrieved from http://identify.whatbird.com/obj/196/overview/Western_Tanager.aspx

Mahatma Gandhi Quotes. (n.d.) Goodreads. Quotable Quotes. Retrieved from https://www.goodreads.com/quotes/24499-be-the-change-that-you-wish-to-see-in-the

Anderson, Mac & Parker Sam. (2006). 212-The Extra Degree. The Walk the Talk Company.

Murphy,W. (2016). Everlasting God. On Youtube [Audio file]. Retrieved from https://www.youtube.com/watch?v=3PzphkAw8Co

Wachob, J. (2010). The Secret of Health for Both Mind and Body. Retrieved from https://www.mindbodygreen.com/0-1324/The-Secret-of-Health-for-Both-Mind-and-Body.html

Anderson, A.R. (2015). Life has many ways of testing a person's will. Retrieved from http://www.amyreesanderson.com/blog/life-has-many-ways-of-testing-a-persons-will/#.Wz1FfdJKg2w

Copquin, C.G. (2012). Life is what happens while we're not checking facts. Retrieved from https://www.huffingtonpost.com/claudia-gryvatz-copquin/gilda-radner_b_2231040.html

Rowling, J.K. (2017). Pass It On.com. Retrieved from

https://www.passiton.com/inspirational-quotes/6595-rock-bottom-became-the-solid-foundation-on

Bhandari, R (2017). The New York Times: Nepal Bars Solo Climbers from Mount Everest. Retrieved from https://www.bbc.com/news/world-asia-42521138

ACKNOWLEDGMENTS

I thank God for every experience encountered along my journey. The downward spiral was intense, scary, and sometimes seemed unfair. I can honestly say, if I had to do it all again, I would not change a thing. This journey has left its mark on my life. It has influenced who I am. But it would not have been possible without my village. To my family and friends, without you, I would not be. You have breathed life into me, dusted me off after falls, and loved me to life. Thank you!

To my mom, Jeannette, my best girl, we got this! Thank you for being a constant part of my WE.

To my Madear, Edna, you continue to show me how a lady lives and loves. I cherish you!

To my younger siblings, Dameon, Demetrius, and Aaliyah. I hope I can model both what to do and what not to do. You will make your own mistakes, but trust me, some of them honestly are not worth the time! Yolanda, big sis, daddy is proud! I love you all.

To my nieces, nephew and God children, Kylii, Khloe, Kristian, Matthew, and Ethan you truly are the future and I look forward to what you make of it. Watching your growth inspires me to keep moving forward no matter how hard it seems.

To my closer than friends crew, thank you for not asking permission to love me. I needed you and you were there! Andre, Anita, Dee, Denise, Donetta, Jolanda, Kenyatta, La'Ketta, Robyn, Rashaan, Theresa, and Sydney. Thank you for listening, keeping my secrets, and supporting me through the process.

Bishop Burt and Pastor Pat, your presence in my life is a constant reminder that God will never leave me alone. Greater New Birth Pastors and members, your prayers and concern loved me to health. Bless you all.

To my first responders:

Dr. Matthews, thank you for calling me in. You saved my life. Dr. Leila Jerome Clay, little sister, you holding my hand every step of the way kept me sane. I love you. Dr. Puffer, Jamie, and the amazing oncology team thank you for being the best in field. Dr. Heffez, I got it. It was not a migraine! But you truly are the best. My all-star medical team rocks!

The journey of authorship has been amazing. Dr. Lance Secretan and Author Kim Lock, your mentorship through this process has been priceless. To all my fellow Eagles – let's soar!

The last shall be first and the first will be last. To my Sweetie, Clark, my personal Superman – Dwayne McAlister, Sr. you were my sweetest surprise. Thank you for supporting me through this roller coaster called life. Thank you for a new Day 1 and every day after.

To my brothers and sisters experiencing Leukemia or any other type of cancer. Stay strong and do not give up. And those who have been below bottom, look up. Better can be yours. And if you are still singed from the flames along your walk through hellish situations, I applaud you. You survived.

To everyone who took time to read my journey and experience my pain. Thank you. It is my sincere hope that something was said that inspired you and gave you hope. Please know that you too can survive: **ONE MILE BELOW BOTTOM –** KEEPING YOUR JOY IN HELL.

ABOUT THE AUTHOR

Denisha Tate is a business coach, facilitator, and guide. She has been recognized as a Woman of Influence, by the Milwaukee Business Journal and featured on broadcasts such as TBN's Joy in Our Town. Denisha's personal mission is to inspire others. As lead consultant of Denisha Tate & Associates LLC, she empowers others to be their best self. Devastating life experiences, including major medical conditions, have taken Denisha to the edge. Those experiences taught her, when faced with a circumstance bigger than any crisis you have ever managed personally, you must learn to rely on sources beyond your control. She believes, overcoming trials is a team sport and a major player on her team, must be Joy. Whether a training group of 10 or an audience of 2,000 Denisha lights a fire of hope and inspiration that makes others want to LIVE LOVE. For more information about her visit www.DenishaLeads.com